To Roger
Best Wishes from

Deep France

Cave Life in France series

Deep France

Tales from the Loir

*William Glover with illustrations
and photography by Aprille Glover*

Writers Club Press
New York Lincoln Shanghai

Deep France
Tales from the Loir

Writers Club Press
an imprint of iUniverse, Inc.

For information address:
iUniverse
2021 Pine Lake Road, Suite 100
Lincoln, NE 68512
www.iuniverse.com

All photographs and artwork by Aprille Glover

ISBN: 0-595-25392-X

Printed in the United States of America

To Virginia Walker

*Je ne m'intéresse plus qu'à ce qui est vrai,
sincère, pur, large, en un seul mot, l'Authentique.*

Marcel Pagnol

Contents

List of Illustrations

La France Profonde

The local Gendarmes cruise our village every afternoon but usually there is no need to look for criminals. Their job is more to find out what is going on in their jurisdiction. The Gendarmes always travel in pairs and are sometimes called *les poulets* (chickens) or *les hirondelles* (swallows) because of this pairing characteristic. But the cute little names belie the atmosphere when these tall muscular men in commando sweaters stop to investigate a small gathering of residents. They are well acquainted with Monsieur Jean and Le P'tit Jules but it is the pretty young *parisienne* that has attracted their interest.

As they approach the group they formally pull out note pads and pencils before demanding the names and addresses. Jean replies, "My name in Jean Montambaux and I live on the route to Vendôme in Saint Rimay." Le P'tit Jules says that, "My name is André Desneux and I live on the rue des Plantes in Saint Rimay." The policeman stares at the pretty young lady. In a little girl voice she says, "My name is Zoulika Beaumonoir and I live in Paris but my husband and I are restoring a home here in Lavardin." The policeman records the information then stares intently at her. "Can I see your papers, *s'il vous plaît*." Monsieur Jean responds immediately, "Fuck you and your papers" and Zoulika stares at him in horror. Things don't work like this in Paris and the young man glares at Jean before responding, "If we can't see your papers, can we at least have a *petit verre*." This is *la France profonde* (deep France) and even a little joke is celebrated with wine.

The policemen and Monsieur Jean were engaged in a little cinema for the benefit of Zoulika but everyone is happy when they head off to the nearest cave to share a bottle and tell the policemen the latest news of the village. The fact that the Gendarmes drink with the local residents doesn't make this deep France. For the Gendarmes, this is a daily public relations duty in this remote river valley. It is deep France because that *petit verre* (a drink) is part of the social glue that binds people here closely to each other and to the land.

Deep France is a concept difficult to grasp and can be as elusive to those raised in Paris or the larger cities as to an American. It is not a place or a person but rather a way of life that follows the ancient traditions. However, it is more than just a connection to the past. It is a kind of a rhythm of life tuned to the seasons and the land. It is a rhythm that has existed for hundreds of years.

It is easier to identify than to explain. When a proud father wets the lips of his newborn son with a Grand Cru Bordeaux to ensure that the child will grow up to appreciate the fine wines of France, that is *la France profonde*. As a foreigner, I see it in little things but I am sure that I miss more than I see. I see it when a farmer hands me eggs that are still warm from the hen and smiles with satisfaction when I hand him ten francs. I see it when a whole village shows up to help a farmer harvest his grapes for the season. I see it when families spend a day in the woods gathering wild mushrooms. I see it when my neighbors gather dandelions for salad or the stinging nettles called *ortie* for soup. I see it when families gather around the fireplace to roast chestnuts and drink a *vin nouveau* called *Bernache*. I see it in the spring when Maurice Cheron gathers the acacia flower to make donuts and the P'tit Jules gathers lime blossoms to make tea. I see it in May when Monsieur Jean and Monsieur Janvier lead us through the valleys and plains of the *bas vendômois* in search of the young shoots of the wild plum tree to make an aperitif called *pousse d'épine*. I see it in June when friends gather snails and again in July when they gather green walnuts to make *vin noix*.

I see it in the fall when a farmer slaughters a pig and the whole family works for days making blood sausage, rillets, rillons, andouilles and smoked ham. I see it in the winter when eighty-year-old couples dance and sing all night in celebration of Saint Vincent. I see it in the summer when young and old sit around a huge bonfire to watch it burn all night.

I can't define deep France but I recognize it when I see it. This book is a record of my glimpses into a France profound.

Spring

The first evidence of spring is the appearance of flowers. Small yellow narcissuses start popping up in protected spaces at the beginning of March. By mid-March, yellow daffodils and multi-colored primavera takeover and announce the coming of light and longer days. By the end of the month, plum and cherry trees begin to bloom white and pink, giving the countryside a feminine touch. By the first of April, bright-eyed tulips replace the daffodils and the fields of green become speckled with yellow dandelions. By mid-April the countryside is bright yellow with blooming crops of *colza* (rape seed) while flowering bushes of *fuchsia* and *ajonc* add a deeper eggyoke color. By May apple and pear trees are blooming pink and white but bright yellow is still the dominant color. Wildflowers sprinkle the hills and valleys with white, purple, red and gold up until the end of May, but it is the *bouton d'or* (buttercup) that defines spring. The last flower of spring, blooming like an elegant dessert, is the vanilla-scented acacia.

The traditions of spring in the French countryside are almost as perennial as the blooming flowers. We gather dandelions for salad in early March. We harvest clusters of the sweet acacia for beignets in late May. We bottle white wine in April and rosé wine in May. We make *pousse d'épine* and *feuille de pêcher* at the end of May. There is a wine festival every weekend for tasting last year's vintage and very little work is done at this time of the year.

The holidays chain together in one long bridge of festivals, *dégustations*, parties and day-long dinners. It is the first of May. Why not take the week off and gather *muguets* (lily of the valley) for good luck? Since Armistice Day is on the eighth, why not bridge the holiday with Ascension and Pentecost?

Spring is the time for opening your cave and uncorking one of those unlabeled bottles with a group of men in overalls standing around a moldy barrel. All eyes follow the bottle as it fills the small wine glasses. It is time to show your true value as a man and identify the *cépage* (variety of grape). One man says that it is a Vouvray but another says no, it is a *pinot blanc de la region*. Another says it is a *chenin* while some agree it is blanc d'Anjou. The chuckling of a tall man in overalls draws the attention of the group as the debate continues. Then everyone stops and waits in silence as he says "non, non, non." He swirls the liquid in his glass and issues the verdict. "It is a white wine." I marvel at the profound wisdom of this man.

It is spring.

A Country Boy Can Survive

Hank Williams, Jr. sings about how a country boy can run a trotline, skin a deer and do whatever to survive. He extols the virtues of the country boy. I don't know the real name of the song but the familiar refrain that keeps popping into my head is "a county boy can survive." I am not sure that it is true anymore. Recent studies of the rural South indicate that many young people have no idea how to cook a potato or that French fries are made from potatoes.

During the great depression people had to live off the land but I am not sure that Americans have ever truly learned the concept. I can remember when I was five years old kicking over toad stools every morning with my friends in South Georgia. It was great fun because they were poisonous and something akin to an axis of evil. Fifty years later while escorting some French visitors through the back roads of Georgia, they excitedly demanded that I stop, because they wanted to gather for dinner the same toadstools that I used to kick over as a child. They were genuinely surprised that I thought they were poisonous.

No one lives off the land like the French. They eat mushrooms, snails, frogs, and everything that comes out of the water. Chestnuts and walnuts are everywhere in early fall and acacia flowers make great beignets in the spring. In the summer there are wild strawberries, blackberries and wild plums. Even in the middle of winter there are great treats to gather from the land. The season to harvest wild *mâche* and dandelions for making salads is February and early March.

Last week our friend Christine Montambaux invited us to dinner for *crêpes* that are traditionally eaten in February. The tradition is to eat *crêpes* on the second day of February, which is the day of Chandeleur, but, like the *galettes* of Epiphany, they are consumed all month long. *Crêpes* were traditionally cooked over the fire in a cast iron frying pan with a four-foot handle. Christine and her mother, Eliane, decided to make the *crêpes* over the fire to show us how it was done in the old days. In keeping with tradition, they spent the day up on the plain in the vineyards gathering *pissenlit* and wild mâche for our salad.

In France, it is not just the country boys who know how to survive on the land. My neighbors are Parisians who only visit their cave a few times a year, but I am constantly surprised at how much they know about the land and traditions of the countryside. Pierre is an architect who specializes in building bridges all over France. He is originally from this region but has not lived here for many years. His girlfriend is from Paris but she also seems to know the lore of the land. They know the names and uses of plants, herbs, trees and flowers like a Native American medicine man. One evening they were being bitten by bugs, so Pierre went over to a bush and pulled off some leaves and rubbed them on their ankles. He told me it was citronella. The leaves smelled just like the expensive candles that we have been buying to chase mosquitoes.

Everyone gathers dandelions to make salad and acacia flowers to make beignets. Monsieur Jean harvests a wild stinging nettle called *ortie* to make soup and young sprouts of a plum tree to make an aperitif call *pousse d'épine*. My friends from Nantes find wild mushrooms growing on the side of the road. No one lives on honey buns at the local convenience store in France. A country boy can still survive here.

Dandelion Salad

Gather the dandelion leaves before the plant flowers. After the plant flowers, it is too late and the dandelion is not edible. The best time for harvesting the wild dandelion is during the month of February and early March. The best place to find them is in the vineyards but they grow everywhere. Wild mâche also sprouts about the same time in the vineyards and makes a good compliment to the dandelions.

Ingredients:
Vinegar
Rapeseed oil (canola oil)
Salt
Pepper
Hard-boiled egg
Dandelions and Mâche

Directions:
Dissolve the salt and pepper in the vinegar (salt and pepper will not dissolve in oil). Add three parts of oil for each part of vinegar. Pour the vinaigrette in a salad bowl. Add the washed dandelions and mâche. Dice the hard boiled egg and place on the leaves. Toss when ready to eat.

Variation:
Instead of using rapeseed oil, chop and cook bacon in a frying pan. Use the bacon fat instead of the rapeseed oil to make the vinaigrette. Use the bacon to compliment the egg.

Maurice

Some people call me the space cowboy, yeah
Some call me the gangster of love
Some people call me Maurice...
          The Joker by Miller/Ertegun/Curtis

This small, wiry man in his mid-sixties with his incomprehensible deep France *patois* and large ears hardly seems the type to merit the name, *gangster of love*, but nothing could be more accurate. One of the ladies in the village tells me that all the women love Maurice Cheron and that he has left a trail of broken hearts a mile long in this community. One of the reasons for his popularity with the ladies is that he loves them, all of them. Plus his love for dancing endears him to many. I have seen him at three o'clock in the morning going full speed at the local drunken barn dances.

I also see him at seven o'clock in the morning, running, speed walking or cycling. He is indefatigable.

Aside from love and leisure, Maurice works with ceaseless energy at the seasonal traditions of the countryside. He is a longtime resident of Lavardin and a man who lives those traditions. He is originally from the Sarthe region, which is even deeper France than the Loir Valley. Following him around is a good way of learning about the ancient traditions of rural France.

I recently saw Maurice with a basket picking *mauvaises herbes* (weeds). As it turns out, he was not picking but harvesting weeds, or at least one weed in particular. He was gathering *pissenlits* to make salad. *Pissenlits* are what we call dandelions in English. During the month of February and the early part of March the young tender shoots are used along with vinaigrette, garlic, croutons, cheese and hard-boiled eggs to make salads. By the end of March the leaves are too hard and bitter to be used as salad but the dandelions sprout again in the early fall and can again be harvested. Some people cook the leaves as a replacement for spinach or use the young flower buds to replace asparagus points. *Pissenlit* is also called *dent-de-lion, couronne de moine*, and *salade de taupe*. *Dent-de-lion* (lion's tooth) is probably the source of our word dandelion. It is easily recognized by its bright yellow flowers.

Pissenlit is a diuretic and has been prized for its medicinal assets for hundreds of years. It is supposed to reduce blood pressure, eliminate excess body fluids and dissolve gallstones among other things. It was once customary to make wine from dandelions. I have not seen this done yet, but Maurice may yet lead me to find this tradition.

Here is my translation of a recipe for dandelion wine that I found on the Internet. It is an aperitif that cleanses and heals. The only caution given is for people with problems involving the kidneys, heart, bladder or the intestines. That probably includes most humans but maybe your mother-in-law would like a bottle.

Vin de Pissenlit

Plantes sauvages médicinales, Anny Schneider, Editions de l'Homme, 1999.

Ingredients:
4 liters of boiling water
4 liters of fresh dandelion flowers
1 zest of orange
1 zest of lemon
1.75 kg of sugar
A large piece of ginger root (about 4 cm)
1 soupspoon of beer yeast
1 small slice of bread.

Instructions:
1. Pour boiling water on the flowers (preferably in a bowl) and allow to soak for 3 days while covered. Stir from time to time.
2. Filter the liquid and boil it for 30 minutes while adding the sugar, the zests and small pieces of the ginger.
3. After the liquid cools, put it in a large jar.
4. Spread the yeast on the bread and put it on top of the liquid.
Cover the jar and allow it to ferment.
5. When the wine stops foaming, put it in a sealed barrel (California oak will do) and wait 3 months before putting in bottles.

The Egg

I come to the farm of Guy and Raymonde Lory once a week to buy eggs and goat cheese. Cheese is available when the goats aren't feeding the young, which seems to be about two months out of the year. But eggs are available almost every week and they are special. Even *les oeufs biologiques* that we buy in the supermarkets can't match these eggs. The large dark, yellow yokes are full of flavor and can make an omelet a gourmet treat.

The best time to visit is after five o'clock. Guy and Raymonde work in the fields and vineyards all day long despite their seventy something years. I park on the side of the road and walk down the steep muddy path to the old mill that they use as a home and farm. The stream that powered the mill has been diverted to run by the side of the old mill house but there is still evidence of the old streambed under the house. The house was flooded last week when the stream flooded its banks. Half of the house is devoted to farm animals. Chickens, dogs and goats scurry out of the way as I negotiate the slippery path to the front door.

When I knock on the door I hear a noise inside that I interpret as an invitation to enter. The door opens into the kitchen where Guy and Raymonde are sitting at a table entertaining some relatives from Saint Arnoult. The house has the warm earthy smell of the farm and the atmosphere of hospitality. When Guy extends his right hand, it feels like a hunk of dry, rough leather but his grip is warm and gentle. The gentle grip may be the result of his missing fingers but I suspect it is more of a reflection of the sweet, gentle character of these hobbit-like people. Four kisses on the cheek for Raymonde and handshakes for the relatives completes the local etiquette for introductions. Like most of the farmers in our neighborhood, they are small hardy people in their mid seventies who seem to be melting into the ground that they have cultivated for so many years. Guy and Raymonde both walk with a sideways rocking motion because arthritis has stiffened the knees. But they show no signs of pain. They are all smiles and I have the warm sensation of being welcome. Guy broadcasts the latest Monsieur Jean story. He sounds like there is a small person yelling from the back of his throat. This phenomenon results from trying to talk while smiling. Guy never stops smiling.

Although out of sequence, we talk about the weather for several minutes. All conversations in the Loir Valley start with a brief discussion of the weather. "*Ah! De sale temps. Il pluie, pluie, pluie. C'est terrible.*" A *petit verre* usually follows the weather. Guy rhetorically asks if I would like a glass of wine. He pours me a tall glass of the pink liquid that I already know to be the dry, flinty *pineau d'aunis* wine from their vineyard. Guy tells me that this is the last of his wine. He is giving up winemaking and is burning the vines for heat this winter. The vines are old and they don't wish to replant. I am a little surprised but this seems to be happening more and more in the countryside of France. These little farmers in their seventies and eighties are the last of a breed of people carrying on the old country traditions.

Raymonde tells me that there is no cheese because the newborns are still nursing. Egg production is also down because of the humidity. Chickens don't lay eggs when it is too wet. Guy goes to check the egg supply and tells me that he only has eleven eggs. I am satisfied with that many but he tells me to wait few moments. He waddles across the barnyard to the chicken shed and returns a few minutes later. He extends his cupped hands to me and I take its contents. It is an egg. It is warm.

Caves

Two caves near the *mairie* (Mayor's Office) collapsed last night. Rescue efforts commenced immediately but all the wine was lost. A search for survivors will commence next week. Of course it's a *blague* (joke), but two wine caves did collapse two weeks ago. Since then there have been some landslides and our own little goat path is collapsing on one end. It has rained everyday since September and the excess water has caused cave-ins all over the Loir and Cher. Jean Michel, my neighbor and a fellow cave dweller, stopped to discuss the problem this morning. He says the large boulders and tons of earth plugging the caves on the *Rue des Caves de Violette* makes him think more about living in a cave. I have been thinking about it too, but our cave is high and dry and I can see no structural problems. However, one of the caves nearby had a two thousand pound chunk of stone fall out of the ceiling and crush a refrigerator flat. Monsieur Jean[1] and I had been in that cave just the day before. Jean warned me that the ceiling was dangerous but I could see nothing unusual in the cracks and fissures that all caves seem to have. The boulder fell right after we walked outside. I am now a believer in the expertise of Monsieur Jean.

When I first moved to Lavardin three years ago, I was looking for a cave that Aprille could use as an art studio. Everyone was very nice and said they would keep an eye open for anything that came up for sale. After a year and a half of searching, I was giving up hope. Artists are revered in France but finding a cave for Aprille just didn't seem to be a pressing problem. The attitude seems to be that caves are for wine not artists. I mentioned to Monsieur Jean one day that our *maison troglodyte* (cave home) was too warm to store wine. Within a week, he found me a cave that Aprille uses as a studio and I use to store wine.

Everything changed when word got out that my wine might be getting warm. People were stopping me on the street to offer me a key to their cave for temporary storage and many came forward with caves for sale or rent. This is an example of the priority of wine in our little corner of France. Madame Lallier told Aprille that Lavardin was a real party town twenty years ago. She said everyone had a wine making cave with a *pressoir* and a few rows of vines. Afternoon wine tastings in the caves were a daily event. It makes me feel good to know that I am helping to preserve this tradition.

Actually the people were right about caves not being a good place for an art studio. The cave we rented was too humid for most of Aprille's supplies and equipment. When we moved her to a building in Montoire, I had to start searching for another place for my wine. The people of Lavardin were so concerned about my soon-to-be orphaned wine, that everyone was again offering a space in their caves. But Monsieur Jean was the most animated. He insisted that I have my own cave in case the owner dies and I

---

[1] Monsieur Jean is Jean Montambaux. He owns a wine cave on the Rotte aux Biques and has become our best friend in France. He is prominent in *Cave Live in France.*

have to fight with the heirs over what is actually my wine. Since I paid no more than seventy-five cents per bottle for most of it, I am not particularly concerned. I suspect that Jean is not concerned either. He just wants to go cave shopping which entails driving around all day meeting people and sharing a glass of wine at each stop. Aprille and I did this last year. We drove around for two weeks drinking wine all day long. This cave is to too wet. That cave is too small. Those caves are too dangerous. These caves are too expensive.

Monsieur Jean just loves to shop for caves. But his persistence has paid off. Pierre Caps, the mayor of Saint Rimay, has a vacant cave in the village of Les Roches l'Eveque but it needs a new door. I can use it for free if I put a door on it. I am quite happy with this arrangement but Jean is not satisfied. He thinks that it is outrageous that I have to pay for the door. But he agrees that it being free is a good deal and it is a good starting point for an American. He still believes that a man ought to have his own cave and this arrangement gives him an excuse to continue our shopping.

I am ready to move the wine and jury-rig the door just to get the problem behind me. But Jean and Pierre will not stand for such gaucheries. The whole process will take at least two more months. It is a small cave (*cavelot*) that sits beside Pierre's cave. It has no name but Pierre's cave has a name and a long history to go with it. It is called *Blue, Blanc, Rouge.* It was the meeting place for veterans of the first Great War and its door was painted blue, white and red like the French flag. Because of those rebellious colors, the Germans who occupied this area during World War II kept a constant watch on this cave. During the fourteenth and fifteenth centuries it was the guard house for one of the gates to the medieval city of La Roche. The rings that the guards used to tie the horses are still carved into the walls. There is a spring somewhere deep in the mountain that flows from a dark tunnel that leads to the dark depths of the underworld. This cave is full of history and mystery but we spend most of our time sitting at a table in the large guardroom near the front discussing the transfer of wine and sipping Vouvray.

It took two months but the door is finally up. We are transferring the wine today. A meeting has been set for three o'clock at *Blue, Blanc, Rouge*. Aprille arrived with a special label for Pierre's *pousse d'épine* that commemorates the deep history of his cave. It looks like a regular wine label but it says *appellation controlée* par Aprille Glover to insure that it is not taken too seriously. We share a bottle of Vouvray and Aprille contributes a bottle of her *Beaume de Venise*. The transfer of the wine takes about five minutes but it was done with the proper reverence and ceremony. Monsieur Jean suggests that I leave a copy of my key on the ledge above the door in case I forget to bring the master. He says that everybody does that. I wonder why I needed the door.

Trôo

Monday was the annual Easter *randonnée pédestre* in Lavardin. It is always held on the Monday after Easter Sunday and is a very popular event. There were 367 participants, which is less than last year, but the weather has been bad all spring so the hiking enthusiasm is still low in the Loir and Cher. Aprille got up very early to help *Les Amis de Lavardin* prepare the *casse-croûte*, which is provided at a point on the trail where the average Frenchman would feel a need for a glass of *vin rouge*. There is nothing like a *coup de rouge* and a ham sandwich to give one energy for the finishing miles. We got started a little late so we were hiking alone for the first couple of miles. Aprille was in high spirits and was talking (lecturing) non-stop about post-modern *fin de siècle* irony or something like that when I had to laugh. Her *bavardage* reminded me of the legend of the singing well of Trôo. When she asked why I was laughing, I told her the story.

A gentleman in the nearby village of Trôo found and married a pretty young girl who made him extremely happy. But after a couple of months of marriage, he discovered that the pretty young thing had one fault. She talked non-stop, even in her sleep. After some months, he was at wits' end, and exclaimed, "If the devil would take you, I would gladly give you away." Suddenly a bolt of lightening from the sky struck the ground in front of them and the devil appeared. The devil who was delighted to see such a pretty young girl said, "I accept your offer" and flew off with the girl in his arms. The girl, instead of being horrified, was delighted that she had someone new to talk to and commenced to drive the devil crazy with her prattle. The devil, understanding his mistake, threw the girl back to the ground where she landed with such force that she made a hole hundreds of feet deep. Having no one to talk to in her hole she commenced to talk with herself and repeat the same things over and over. This same echo can still be heard today when one leans over the mouth of the singing well of Trôo and speaks to the *chanteur*.

Another legend from Trôo is that when *Richard Coeur de Lion* (Richard the Lion Hearted) first contemplated a siege of this fortified city, he said, "*C'est trop haut*" (It is too high). Phonetically, *trop haut* is pronounced TRO O with long O's. It is an odd pronunciation and a very unusual village. In the middle ages it was a troglodyte village of more than four thousand people, most of whom resided in the miles of caves carved into the mountain. Today it is still a cave town but its population is less than five hundred people and one is more likely to hear English spoken than anywhere else in the Vendômois region of France. The English seem to think that they have certain rights to this town since it was originally part of the English Plantagenêt domain in France. Actually the Plantagenêt were more French than English and their title of King of England meant less than being Duke of Anjou. The most famous of the Plantagenêt, Richard the Lion Hearted, Henry II and Eleanor of Aquitaine, are buried just south of here in the *Abbaye de Fontevault*. The English have petitioned to have the tombs moved to England but these English kings and queens had very little to do with England and the French refuse to make the transfer.

It was Richard the Lion Hearted and his Plantagenêt ancestors who built the abbeys, churches and the chateau-fortress at Trôo, but the caves have a history stretching back to the Gallic tribes who used them as a system of defense against the Roman invaders. Today, Trôo offers the best in troglodyte tourism. Visitors can tour an ancient *habitation troglodyte* and visit the miles of Cafort de Lusignan which was successively a cave-fort and quarry in the middle ages, and, more recently, a mushroom farm and community rooms for parties and celebrations. It was in investigating these caves that I found a *gîte* (bed and breakfast) entirely in a cave that visitors could rent for a night, a week or by the month. For anyone interested in living in a cave, a visit to Trôo is a good place to start. The caves in Trôo are classified as a national heritage by the French government.

The *Gîte Troglodytique* is owned by Barbara and Bernard Savaete, Escalier Saint Gabriel, 41800 Trôo, France, Tel. 02 54 72 50 34, E-mail: bandbcave@minitel.net.

May Day

Traditionally, a gift of the small white bell-shaped flower called *muguet* is said to *porter bonheur* (bring good luck). The source of this tradition is hard to pin down but it seems to have started in the 1930s when the communist party sold *muguets* in Paris on the first day of May to raise money. Even though the communists probably started this tradition, it is the capitalists who profit from it. When Claude Chêne, *ladite* Dame de Beaumé, warned me that it was a tradition to give a bouquet of muguets on the first of May, I went shopping. The local Flowers R Us is called Jardiland and they are not communists. Flowers are normally cheap in France but on the first day of May, a small pot of three *muguets* costs about five dollars. I can usually buy a dozen roses for five dollars but the law of supply and demand on this one day of the year is harsh. Fortunately, I paid the price and stocked up. On the morning of the first of May, my neighbor, Madame Lallier, knocked on my door and handed me a bouquet of *muguets* and told me *il porte de bonheur*. I returned the favor and presented my own good luck to her.

Madame Lallier told me that the first of May was a very important holiday in France and that the village would be full of tourists to *faire le pont*. *Faire le pont* literally means to make a bridge. Practically it means to make a long weekend by taking off from work on Friday or Monday. This is not an unusual concept in America where the government normally designates Monday as the official holiday if the real day of celebration falls on an inconvenient day. The French, who usually get five weeks of vacation time, make bridges all year long just by scheduling a day off from work. Americans are lucky to get one week off and they are not expected to take it so they resort to calling in sick on Friday or Monday.

So what happens when the first day of May falls on a Tuesday? In America everybody goes to work; in France everybody gets a four-day weekend. In the States, we are still rooting out communist conspiracies. But France is the land of Jean Jacques Rousseau, the social contract and the Great Revolution. In short, nobody pushes the workers around here. The Revolution gave a kind of power to the people that everyone still fears, even the people. Today, demonstrations and strikes are usually peaceful events that end in compromise.

Ironically, May Day as it is celebrated today comes from America. On 1 May 1886, workers were demonstrating in Chicago for an eight-hour workday when police attacked and killed six of the workers in Haymarket Square. In 1889, the first international union in Paris declared May first as an international working class holiday in remembrance of the Haymarket martyrs.

The most interesting thing about May Day is that it is a completely secular holiday. Most holidays in France have a religious foundation. May Day was originally a pagan celebration of the coming of spring but it was never adapted to the Christian celebrations as were other pagan holidays. Although many cathedrals and churches are built over *dolmens, menhir*s, Roman temples and Celtic holy places, the church had to draw a distinction somewhere. Perhaps May Day's roots in the fertility cults were too much for early Christians to accept and a good place to draw the distinction.

Armistice Day

On 8 May 1945, the American Army liberated Paris. The French celebrate this day every year with parades, ceremonies and memorial speeches. The ancient combatants of Lavardin put on their uniforms and marched to the cemetery with their flags and wreaths for the appropriate memorial services. Three French flags are on display on all government buildings and of course everyone takes another four-day weekend. The following weekend there are parades in every village and town in France. Over seven hundred ancient combatants march in the parade in Montoire.

The month of May seems to be one long holiday and America seems to be a part of all these celebrations. Very few Americans venture into the Loir and Cher but most of the people here have good memories of our GI's. It can be embarrassing when some of these tough guys begin to cry so I don't usually bring up the subject, but today it seems appropriate to ask about it.

My friend, Gaston Cottenceau, asked me to share a glass of wine and I decided to take the opportunity to ask him if he lived in Lavardin during the war. He tells me he was nine years old when Patton's army crossed the bridge with their tanks. He says the GI's were throwing them cigarettes and chewing gum. Gaston, who is a master stonemason, chain smokes Marlboros and has the rugged, cowboy look of the real Marlboro Man so I don't expect him to cry. When his eyes begin to water, I get a little uneasy but I see that it is the smoke that is bothering him more than the emotion. He thinks for a while, then after another drag, he says, "That was the day that I started smoking. It has been almost sixty years and I am still smoking two packs a day." I am completely taken aback and begin to apologize for what my country has done to him. He plays me like a hooked trout for a few minutes before exploding in laughter at my dilemma.

I should have known that he was joking because Gaston dresses up in a GI uniform and drives one the original American Jeeps through the streets of Montoire on these days of liberation. Despite his age, he looks just like an authentic WWII American GI.

Montoire was the village where Marechal Petain shook hands with Adolf Hitler and agreed to surrender. Many French call this the most shameful day in the history of France and refer to it as the collaboration. The older people of this region still tell stories about hiding from the Germans who were hauling off young men and women to work in the factories in Germany. The American soldiers handing out chewing gum and cigarettes were a stark contrast to the German soldiers who took their food and randomly shot people who were a problem.

The people of Montoire didn't even know that the meeting had taken place in their village until long after Hilter had left but they seem to feel responsible anyway. I have traveled all over France and met many nice people but nowhere matches Montoire's hospitality and warmth. Perhaps they feel an obligation to make up for the shameful event that occurred in their town. Visitors can see an exhibit of the events in the old railway station where the meeting took place. One can also visit the tunnel in Saint Rimay where Hitler's train was parked to protect it from American bombers.

Beignets Aux Fleurs d'Acacia

I have been reading about the traditions of the people in the *bas vendômois* and the regions lengthening the Loir River. No traditions run deeper or are more significant than those of food and wine. But when it comes to the subject of desserts, discoveries are even more precious because they are more rare. The French probably eat more varieties of desserts today than in the good old days. Local historians tell me that the traditional desserts of a hundred years ago where probably quiet simple. There were *confitures* and *compotes* that are still enjoyed today but specialties like *la compote de verjus* (made with *muscat* grapes) have all but disappeared. Things like *tartes aux pommes, galettes and crêpes* were reserved for festival days but the children might be treated to something like *pain perdu* (lost bread or French toast) flavored with orange blossoms on a weekly basis. I have now learned that there were seasonal desserts that were so special that they still exist today.

Last May when I was doing a *randonnée pédestre* (hike) with my friends Maurice, Simone and Christine in the village of Molineuf near Blois, my attention was directed to a beautiful and aromatic flower growing high in a tree along the trail. Simone and Christine first spotted the acacia tree as we were leaving the dark path of the woods. They stopped to tell me why these sweet flowers are prized by bees and humans alike. I have seen the word acacia on the jars of honey and I know it is a point of pride for bee-keepers to advertise that their honey is made from acacia flowers. However, I did not know that people eat the flowers too. The acacia flowers grow in bunches like grapes and have a sweet vanilla aroma. Simone told me that you dip the *grappe* (bunch) in a *beignet* (donut) batter and fry it in hot oil.

25

A couple of weeks later, I decided to try it. I stopped on the side of the road where acacia was flowering. The latter part of May is toward the end of the season for the flower but it is still abundant. In a few minutes, I have a sack full of acacia. I make the batter with two eggs, flour, salt, lots of sugar and water. I dip the acacia flowers in the batter and cook it in hot sunflower seed oil. The result is *Beignets Aux Fleur d'Acacia*. It is easy, authentic and traditional. It is also very good.

Acacia Beignets

Ingredients:
Two Eggs
Flour
Salt
Sugar
Grappe d'Acacia[2] (blooms in April and May)
Sunflower seed or canola oil
Directions:
 Make a batter with the two eggs, flour, salt, sugar and water. Let it rest for an hour. Dip the clusters of flowers in the batter and fry in the hot oil. Sprinkle with sugar and serve hot.

---

[2] This flower is not a true acacia. The real acacia is a mimosa. The scientific name for what the French call an acacia is *robinia pseudoacacia*. In America it is called Black Locust and grows in the Appalachian mountain range.

Pousse d'Epine

Pousse means push in French and it is the word used to describe young branches that appear on plants in the spring. For the last two years I have been hearing my neighbors talk about making *pousse d'épine* in the month of May. The words always went a little too quickly to follow. I could follow the ten liters of cabernet sauvignon but I had no idea what two liters of *goutte* meant or what an *épine* was. I later learned that *goutte* was *eau-de-vie* and that *pousse d'épine* was the young shoots of a bush called an *épine*. My friends, Jean Montambaux and his daughter Christine, agreed to include me in the annual ritual of making *pousse d'épine*. Jean said it was very simple. All we need is wine, *goutte*, powdered sugar and young sprouts *d'épine*.

Yesterday, we visited the vineyard of Dominique Norguet and bought the ten liters of cabernet sauvignon. Today we are searching for the tender young shoots of the *épine* tree. I later learned that this is really a kind of wild plum tree. When I was harvesting the shoots, it looked like an ordinary bush on the side of the road. Later in the fall, I saw it bearing fruit. The *épine* pushes new shoots or branches in May and August and these are the two months that you can make *pousse d'épine*.

Jean, Christine and I load baskets and clippers in Jean's Citroën. He engages the hydraulic lifting system that elevates the car and we take off. Only the French could build a car like this. Jean says that it has to be the right height to find the *épine*. We drive down a deserted gravel road near the commune of Paradis and find the épine bushes along side the road. Jean shows me the irregular pattern of leaves on the young shoots and tells me that this is what we need. We fill our baskets with the young shoots and head to St. Rimay where Jean negotiates the purchase of two liters of *eau-de-vie*. He calls it the *goutte* and says that it is eight-years old. We head to Christine's *fermette* to do the mixing. Jean borrowed a small barrel from André (P'tit Jules) Desneux so that I could mix my batch. We haul all of the ingredients into one of Christine's four caves for mixing and aging. The rest is quite simple. First I put the branches of the *épine* in the barrel. Then add the ten liters of cabernet sauvignon and two liters of *eau-de-vie*. The last ingredient is seven hundred grams of powdered sugar. The mixture must be stirred twice a day for about two weeks. After that, it rests tranquil until the middle of July when it is filtered and corked in old champagne or *vin mousseux* bottles. The corked bottles should be stored standing up. It should be served cold or even with an ice cube but it should not be stored in a refrigerator. I left a bottle in my refrigerator and the mixture separated. I have been told that the refrigerator is also bad for wine and will cause it to break down too. *Pousse d'épine* can be stored for years in a 12° C cave and will get better with age. It has the taste of a very fine port and is usually drunk as an aperitif. It is also excellent poured into a half of cantaloupe or melon.

Pousse d'Epine

Ingredients:
10 liters of red or rosé wine
2 liters of eau-de-vie
700 grams of sugar
Shoots from the épine noir
Directions:
Gather the young shoots of the prunnelle (sloe) tree (l'épine noir) in May or August. Put the shoots in a fifteen-liter container. Add the eau-de-vie, wine and sugar. Stir the contents and cover with a clean linen cloth. Stir the contents every day for two weeks to ensure that the sugar is dissolved. Let it sit for about six weeks then bottle it. Serve chilled but do not store in the refrigerator. If stored in a cool, dark environment, it will improve with the years.

Les Journées des Aubepines

Each spring, the Society of the Friends of Marcel Proust and the Friends of Combray sponsor a weekend of activities celebrating the memory of Marcel Proust in the village of Illiers-Combray. *Les Journées des Aubepines* means days of the hawthorns and it is the time of the year that the hawthorns of Marcel Proust's Combray are in full bloom. Mid-May is the time to visit the ancestral home of Marcel Proust's family and to meet the *amateurs* of his work. *Amateur* is the closest word that I can find to the meaning of the English word "fan". I was pleasantly surprised to find the fans of Marcel Proust to be so nice. For some reason, I have concocted an image of Proust fans as snobs but every one that I have met with an interest in Proust has been a delightful surprise.

We were especially delighted to meet two Americans who were there to explore the possibility of recreating a Proustien experience for travelers interested in Marcel Proust. The company is called Great Composer Tours. It was started by Joseph and Cynthia Lawton who have been organizing Biographical Travel Adventures based on the lives of the great composers. They have decided to expand their adventures to literary figures and are looking at Marcel Proust as a subject. We especially enjoyed speaking English for a change and were fascinated with their new business.

The day started with an exposition and presentation of new items to the Proust Museum. After the presentation the guests were allowed to roam around the *Maison de tante Léonie* which is the museum. Afterwards, we were served cider and *amuses bouches* in the garden. We had lunch at *le Florent*, which is the restaurant next to the old grocery that the Proust family owned. The bus tour started at about two-thirty in the afternoon and made a circuit of Proust's Swan's Way and the Guermante Way. We stopped at the *Pré Catalan*[3] and heard passages from Swan's Way about the hawthorns and saw the blossoms at their height. We also made stops at Tansonville, Saint-Eman and the home of Monsieur Vinteuil.

The French have a way of doing these things in such a simple and understated way that it is hard to find fault with their effort. This is a pleasant weekend in the middle of May and something to put on the calendar for next year.

---

[3] The *Pré Catalan* is Swan's garden that Marcel Proust describes in his novel. The literal meaning of *Pré Catalan* is Catalonian field.

Marcel Proust

There is an old Celtic belief that the souls of our ancestors are held captive in plants, animals and other objects when they die. These souls can be lost forever unless a descendant or kindred spirit happens to pass close by and awaken the lost soul. If we happen to recognize the voice of the lost soul, the spell is broken and it is released from its prison of death. Having overcome death they return to share our life. I am now convinced that something like this happened to me.

It has been a dark, wet winter along the swollen Loir River. I have not seen the sun for several months. After a dreary day with the prospect of a depressing morrow, I decided to visit the cave of my friend, Jean Montambaux, with the hope of lifting my spirits. Even the cheerful *ça va-t-il* of Monsieur Jean failed to change my mood but I accepted a *petit verre* of Vouvray nevertheless. As I watched Jean dip one of the rectangular cookies from Brittany called a *petite beurre* in his glass of Vouvray, for some unknown reason, I was tempted to try it myself even though it was something that I had never tried before. No sooner had the Vouvray soaked *petite beurre* touched my palate than a shudder ran through me and I stopped, intent upon the extraordinary thing that was happening to me. An exquisite pleasure had invaded my senses, something isolated, detached, with no suggestion of its origin. And at once the vicissitudes of life had become indifferent to me, its disasters innocuous, its brevity illusory—this new sensation having had on me the effect which love has of filling me with a precious essence; or rather this essence was not in me, it was me. I had ceased now to feel mediocre, contingent, mortal. Whence could it have come to me, this all-powerful joy? I sensed that it was connected with the taste of the Vouvray and the *petit beurre,* but that it infinitely transcended

32

these savors, could not, indeed, be of the same nature. Whence did it come? What did it mean? How could I seize and apprehend it?

And suddenly the memory revealed itself. The taste was that of the a moon pie which my friend Jack Marshall and I ate every day at Patrol Boy camp in Cordele, Georgia, more that forty years ago. We used to dip it in our RC Colas before eating it.

And as soon as I had recognized the taste of the piece of moon pie soaked in RC Cola…immediately the giant moss draped oak trees of St. Simons Island rose up like a stage in my memory. So in that moment all the azaleas in our front yard and everywhere on the island and the marsh grass along the Frederica River and the good folk of the village and their little dwellings and the Methodist church and the whole of St. Simons Island and its surroundings, taking shape and solidity, sprang into being, town and gardens alike, from my little taste of a *petite beurre* soaked in Vouvray.

Marcel Proust readers have already recognized my parody of the extraordinary events leading to his *Remembrance of Things Past*. For Proust it was *petites madeleines* soaked in lime blossom tea that triggered the eight volumes and three thousand pages of his classic novel. To read the real explication of his recollection see *Swan's Way*, Marcel Proust, pp. 48-51.

In my search for the source of the Loir River, I came across the small town of Illiers-Combray. It is a small quiet village nestled between the wheat fields of the Beauce and the gentle valleys of the Perche. It is a few miles southwest of Chartres and about two miles south of the source of the Loir River. It is also the ancestral home of Marcel Proust's family and the central setting of his masterpiece novel. Although he never actually lived there, he did spend some summers in Illiers with his family when he was a child. It was his childhood memories of those visits to Illiers that triggered the eight volumes of his reflections on the past. He describes in exquisite detail the streets, buildings and surroundings of his fictional Combray. Although he changed the names of some things like the name of the village, it exists today very much like he described it. In 1971, the village changed its name from Illiers to Illiers-Combray to take advantage of Marcel Proust's renown.

The first time that I went to the village of Illiers-Combray, I knew very little about Marcel Proust. I was vaguely aware of his masterpiece novel but what little I had read did not interest me too much. He seemed a little too prissy for me. I am more of a Herman Melville type. I would rather be hunting whales to near extinction and sitting on south sea beaches than whining for dozens of pages about how hard it is to wake up in the morning.

I began to take notice of Proust several years ago when I read a book written by Larry McMurtry entitled *The Evening Star*. In that novel, the heroine was an elderly lady who was reading Proust. It was her lifelong dream to finish the eight volumes and she had been working on it all of her life. I later met other people who claimed to be reading Proust in this same Sisyphean way. I always got the sense that these people were toiling in punishment like the man in the Greek myth rolling the boulder uphill for eternity. I have never found anyone who had actually read the whole work and most people have told me that they tried to read Proust but couldn't get through the first volume. Even Aprille, who devours books in huge gulps, told me that she tried to read him when she was much younger but gave up after about two hundred pages. This surprised me because there is nothing that seems to daunt her reading tastes.

At one time I was convinced that reading Proust was a snobbish thing to do and that everyone was doing it to acquire a kind of intellectual ranking. To say "I have read Proust" would be like a mountain climber saying that he had climbed Mount Everest. In fact, it may be harder to read the eight volumes of *Remembrance of Things Past* than to climb the mountain. I don't know of anyone who has finished Proust but many people have climbed the mountain, albeit with teams of Sherpas and bottles of oxygen. It is easy to cheat on the mountain and many climbers have actually been short-roped to the top when they couldn't go any further. Being short-roped means a Sherpa ties a short rope around your waist and pulls you up the last few hundred feet. But there is no way to cheat in the reading of Proust. You have to read it all by yourself.

I bought a copy of, *Swan's Way*, the first of the eight volumes of *Remembrance of Things Past*, to at least get a sense of what Proust is all about. After about ten naps induced by reading, I asked a professor friend to read a little and tell me what he thought. After a couple of days, he gave me the book back. His comment was that "these are some bored ass people." *Swan's Way* is only about 462 pages but finishing it is a formidable task. I would compare it to getting to the base camp of Mount Everest which is no mean task in itself. I now see why it is a lifetime chore to read it all. The question remains of why should anyone do it?

People do it because reading Proust is an infectious and incurable disease. Once you are infected, it is a lifetime struggle to finish. When I told Aprille that I couldn't read Proust without falling asleep and that I didn't believe anyone had actually read the entire eight volumes. I piqued her interest and awoke her Zen spirit. She often says that she is a Zen Buddhist but she is so competitive that it is hard to associate inner peace with her will to win. The end result is that we now spend long hours discussing Proust and drinking lime-blossom tea with our *petites madeleines.* Just this morning I said "Dear, do you remember when Proust said:

> *...an invisible bird was striving to make the day seem shorter,*
> *exploring with a long-drawn note the solitude that pressed it*
> *on every side, but it received at once so unanimous an answer,*
> *so powerful a repercussion of silence and of immobility, that*
> *one felt it had arrested for all eternity the moment which it*
> *had been trying to make pass more quickly".*

Her reply was "Of course, but you have to remember that Proust was a master of nuance and subtlety and those words can't be taken literally." "Indeed, quite so".

Since I have taken up the task of reading Proust myself, I am even considering taking on the whole eight volumes. My friend, Mike McBride, who is a retired diplomat living in Paris has been reading Proust in the original French. This is sort of like climbing the north face of Everest without oxygen or Sherpas. I am quite happy that I have reached the base camp. Whether I go any higher depends on many things. But in the main, it depends on whether I can find the audiotapes for the other seven volumes.

Honoré de Balzac
La Grand Bretèche

The city of Vendôme recently celebrated the bicentennial of the birth of Honoré de Balzac who was born in Tours, France on May 20, 1799. The great French writer, who wrote over ninety novels, spent six years at the Collège des Oratoriens in Vendôme, France from 1807 to 1813. The memories of his days in Vendôme stayed with him for a long time and he eventually wrote three books in which Vendôme was the setting. *Louis Lambert* was an autobiographical novel that described life in Vendôme and the first part of *Lys Dans La Vallée* was set in this ancient village. However, La *Grande Bretèche* is the novel that is most notable for Vendôme. *La Grand Bretèche* is also the name of a house in Vendôme that exists in its original state today. The French often have names for their houses, farms, neighborhoods and communities that have origins deep in the past. It is just as fascinating for me to learn that no one knows why a name exists as to hear the actual story of where it came from. When you don't know the actual source of the name you can make up you own romantic notions. This house sits in the center of Vendôme and backs up to the Loir River. In front of the house, there is a high stonewall with large, wooden, double doors and arched stonework above. Behind these doors, one enters the courtyard. This eighteenth century, four-story, ivy covered stone house is about fifty feet back from the stone wall. The thick, green ivy gives the house a dark, somber look. The ivy covers the whole front of the house except for the dark, unlit windows which look like hollow eye sockets. There is a ghostly look to this place, especially at night, and its history is also darkly dramatic.

The story as told by Balzac is that during the Napoleonic Wars, in the early part of the nineteenth century, a wealthy merchant and his pretty young wife occupied this house. A young Spanish nobleman, who was captured during one of these wars, was sent to Vendôme to live on his word of honor not to escape. The Spaniard and the merchant's wife fell in love and carried on an affair in her bedroom. The Spaniard would swim across the river each night and climb up to her bedroom. The merchant, who suspected this affair, surprised the lovers one day. The wife hid the Spaniard in a closet. When the merchant entered the room, he went straight for the closet but his wife asked him not to open it. When he insisted, she said, "If you really love me, you will not open that door." The merchant said "Okay, I will not open the door if you will swear by the Virgin Mary that there is no one behind the door." The wife who was devoutly religious swore that no one was behind the door. The merchant called a brick mason and had him promptly brick up the closet door. In order to protect the honor of his lover, the Spaniard never cried out for help nor did the wife reveal his presence. The Spaniard slowly died behind the brick wall. Balzac now writes for Sesame Street.

I met my friend Claude Rey at the Balzac seminar and she invited me to go with her and her husband, Francis, to an outdoor play based on *La Grande Bretèche* story. It was to be performed in the courtyard of the house. We drove to the center of Vendôme to find it. It had been raining off and on all day and now it was beginning to turn cool. With cool, reflective moisture dripping off stonewalls and narrow cobblestone streets, we made our way to the portals of this house called *La Grande Bretèche*. At any minute I was expecting a man in a horse drawn cart to come by yelling, "Bring out your dead." An expectant group of patrons waited outside the large wooden doors murmuring among themselves. Eventually the doors opened to reveal the candle lit courtyard with the actors posed in their nineteenth century costumes. The actors stood like marble statues while the audience found seats in folding chairs arranged in parallel arcs. When everyone was seated, the first scene commenced with a soliloquy of a young man pacing in the courtyard and talking about how much he enjoyed using the courtyard and how peaceful it was. After the soliloquy, a Notary approached the young man and informed him that he would have to leave and could no longer use the courtyard. The young man asked why and the story of *La Grande Bretèche* was told by the answers of the Notary and other characters who were questioned by the young man. The play was basically a narrative of the story told by various readers, but with the ivy-covered house as a backdrop and the costumed actors reading the script, it worked extremely well. Just standing in the dark in front of *La Grande Bretèche* is all the atmosphere needed.

In celebration of the bicentennial of the birth of Balzac, the town of Vendôme sponsored a series of expositions, conferences, animations and spectacles. The festivities culminated with a grand banquet in the court-yard of the former *Collège des Oratoriens* that is now the *Hôtel de Ville* (city hall) and *Lycée Ronsard*. There is a permanent exhibit at the Office of Tourism, where books, pamphlets and other souvenirs can be purchased. There is also a self-guided walking tour of the city where you can see the actual homes, chateaux and other landmarks of the Balzac novels. For information in English, contact the *Alliance Française* where a warm reception is always provided.

Vouvray

Practically every encounter in France, be it social or be it commercial, requires a proffered glass of something. I might also add that it is mandatory to accept the proffer. Monsieur Jean and Maurice came by to help unload some wood and I made the offer to have a glass of Vouvray in my cave. When I filled the glasses, we clinked and sipped. Their reaction was surprising. Monsieur Jean said the equivalent of "wow" and Maurice turned the bottle around to read the label. The bottle's label read Vouvray, 1990. Evidently, the two great years for the Vouvray region were 1989 and 1990. When Maurice asked for a second glass, Monsieur Jean teased him a little because Maurice rarely has time for a second glass. Maurice responded that that was true but this was not the vinegar that Monsieur Jean served in his cave. Maurice rarely lets anyone top him so he insisted that we go to his cave to compare his stock with mine. Being a sporting man myself who loves this kind of competition, I accepted. When

Maurice disappeared down one of those dark corridors with his foot long brass key, I knew he was going for the good stuff. He brought back an unlabeled bottle and poured us a glass of its light golden liquid. It was excellent and I correctly guessed that it was a 1990 Vouvray. What a duel! Monsieur Jean decided to enter the competition and invited me down to his cave to test his waters. We had a rosé from the Touraine, a Vouvray and a glass of *pousse d'épine*. Monsieur Jean believes that drinking a lot of good wine is better that drinking a little bit of great wine.

The wines of Vouvray are made from the chenin grape. This *cépage* is sometimes called *Pineau blanc de la Loire* or *Pineau de la Loire*. This variety produces two basic types of wines within the Vouvray appellation. *Vins effervescents* are the sparkling wines of the champagne genre. *Vins tranquilles* are the non-sparkling wines. All of the Vouvray wines have a natural tendency to become effervescent and are amenable to the traditional method of making a sparkling wine. The result is a light but spirited wine that is faithful to the *terroir* of Vouvray. There are two types of sparking Vouvray. One is called *pétillant* and is less bubbly than the *mousseux*, which has more carbonation. These wines should be served at about 8°C or 45°F. They can be served as an aperitif or with dessert. They are an excellent buy at a fraction of the cost of a bottle of Champagne.

The non-sparkling wines of Vouvray are either *sec* (dry), *demi-sec* or *moelleux* (sweet) according the year and, above all, the amount of sun they received during the season. All of these wines can be drunk immediately and are very good in their younger years. However, they can also be held for many years and get better each year. Some of the great years can be held for many decades but the winemakers of this region insist that it is not an aging process. They refer to the storage as a ripening process that produces some tastes of ripe quinces and acacia while remaining fruity and fresh. The sweet wines have an amber color in their youth that turns to gold as they mature. These sweet wines are possible because in the autumn, at harvest time. the winemaker waits for the grapes to over-ripen and harvests them by hand selecting only the most mature of the crop.

This kind of triage is called *tris successifs*. It is this over ripening that gives these wines their sweetness. These wines should be served at 12ºC or 55ºF. This is room temperature if you live in a cave. Most caves in the Loir Valley maintain a constant temperature of 12ºC. They are perfect for storing and drinking Vouvray.

Most of the winemakers in Vouvray will sell their wine in *cubi (cubitainer)*. These large cubic plastic containers are often available at the vineyard but can also be purchased at most *hypermarchers*. Like most new white wines, April is the first month that it can be bottled. Young wine has a natural effervescence that will blow the cork out of the bottle if corked before it has fully settled. After transporting a cubi of wine to your cave, you should wait two or three days before bottling. Corks and corking machines are available everywhere in France. You can buy bottles but it is surprising how many you can collect if you are a diligent consumer. A very good Vouvray can be purchased for about fifteen francs per liter. Even after paying for a good cork, the cost is generally less than two dollars per bottle. Vouvray is one of the outstanding bargains in France.

Muscadet

When Monsieur Jean invited me down to his cave for a *p'tit verre*, I contributed a bottle of Muscadet *sur lie* that my friends from Nantes had brought me the week before. Jean was very impressed with the Muscadet. He said it was *très délicat et très fin*. As we were praising this bottle, Gilbert came by and he was also impressed with it. Gilbert, who is usually in a hurry to get back to work, asks for another glass. When you don't want too much wine you lift your glass to lift the spout of the bottle. Gilbert did something that I have never seen before. As Monsieur Jean was pouring, he looped his forefinger over the spout of the bottle to keep him from stopping the pour. This very delicate wine from Nantes created a festive atmosphere and resulted in a prayer from Monsieur Jean. While lifting his glass above his head he recited his mass: *Il est clair; il n'y a pas de dépôt; tu n'en veux pas; toi non plus. Amen à boire.*[4]

---

[4] It is clear; there is no deposit; you do not wish it for them; nor for yourself. Amen, drink up.

I generally find that wines of a specific region taste better when you are in that region. A rosé from Provence is not nearly as good when consumed in the colder climates of the north of France. A gamay from the Touraine wouldn't be right on the beaches of the Mediterranean and you wouldn't want to drink a Bordeaux in Burgundy. Wines reflect the *terroir* of their regions and always taste better in their proper atmosphere. The one wine that might be an exception is Muscadet. It can be found on every wine list in France and it is even available in the States. Its *terroir* is connected to the sea so every menu with seafood is complimented by the Muscadet wine. It is the most popular white wine in France. Over a hundred million bottles are sold each year.

The best of this wine is the Muscadet *sur lie*. It is made by leaving it in the barrel with its dregs. Normally wine is separated from its dregs at least three times by drawing off the wine in the top of the barrel and allowing it to age in clean barrels. By leaving the wine in the barrel on top of its dregs(*lie*), the best and most natural wine is produced. It also allows early bottling which produces a light carbonation in the form of microscopic bubbles that give the wine a special freshness.

Like many good things in France, there is an ancient tradition behind the *sur lie* method of making wine. When a winemaker's daughter became engaged to be married, he would set aside a barrel for the wedding called the *barrique de noce*. This barrel was set aside for the wedding guests and allowed to ferment on its *lies*. The wine turned out to be so good that this method became a tradition with the Muscadet wines.

Muscadet is a very fine and elegant white wine whose color tends to be more of a very pale yellowish gold with reflections of green. It has been an AOC (*appellation d'origine controlée*) wine since 1937 and is made with a grape called *melon de Bourgogne*. It is a hardy variety of grape that is well suited to the regional *terroir* and the climate of the nearby Atlantic Ocean. About half of its production is exported.

Summer

Summer is less complicated than spring. Its palette starts with deep rich green colors before light brown patches are added as the wheat fields mature. Then everything succumbs to bright yellow with the arrival of sunflowers. Summer is the time for roses and geraniums but it is the bright red poppies standing like sentinels at the edge of the wheat fields that defines the summer season.

Bright red cherries ripen in June. Men, women and children hasten to hoist ladders and fill buckets before the birds beat them to the harvest. Cherries are the first fruit of the season and are in such abundance that neighbors give us basket loads for eating chilled in the cave or for making *le clafoutis* and preserves.

Early June is also the season for gathering lime blossoms for making tea. Unfortunately, this is one of those traditions that is disappearing.

Aprille and I went to Illiers-Combray, the village of Marcel Proust's novel, in May to attend a reading and to find where the lime blossoms are gathered. It was lime blossom tea that triggered Proust's remembrance of things past. No one seemed to know where even one *tilleul* (lime) tree could be found. Finally one of the attendees showed us what a lime tree looked like and where they could be found. Aprille went back in early June and harvested the blossoms. Eliane Montambaux showed us how to separate the small tender light green leaves and flower blossoms from the branches and how to dry them for making tea. The P'tit Jules and his wife Jeanine are the only locals we know who still harvest the blossoms for making tea.

Summer is also the season for gathering snails. This too seems to be a dying tradition so I was excited to learn that Christine Montambaux was collecting snails this summer. She promised to show me how to prepare the snails for cooking when she had enough. In early June, snails were scarce but Christine found over a hundred in one day toward the middle of the month and invited me over to watch the process of cleaning and cooking. I now understand why the tradition is disappearing. It is a lot of work.

The backyard vegetable gardens are a lot of work too but this tradition is still very strong. Everyone has a garden that produces huge amounts of fresh tomatoes, carrots, green beans, potatoes and lettuce of all kinds. We find fresh vegetables left at our door several days each week. We even started our own small plot on the hill above the cave this year.

Other traditions are just fun and require no work. On the summer solstice, the village celebrates the *feu de Saint Jean*. This purely pagan holiday involves building a huge fire in the middle of a field then dancing, eating and drinking all night. Many people sit on blankets and watch the fire until sunrise.

A couple of weeks later there is another celebration for French Independence Day with fireworks, sound and light shows, and, of course, eating and drinking.

Summer is also the time for bottling *pousse d'épine*, making walnut wine and corking the last of the Vouvray. Summer is many things, but for me it means sunflowers, *pastis*, eating outside, trips to Provence, rosé wine, cool caves, gypsies and the circus.

Escapade dans le Berry

The *escapade dans le Berry* is a one-day bus trip organized by the village of Saint Rimay to visit the cathedral in Bourges. Aprille and I were invited to go with a group of *campagnards* (country folk) from this small village. We live in the neighboring village of Lavardin but we have friends in Saint Rimay and attend many of their parties and festivals. Even though the two villages are only a couple of miles apart they are vastly different. Lavardin with its chateau and thousand-year-old buildings is classically beautiful and a popular tourist attraction. Saint Rimay on the other hand is truly deep France with the demographics of a typical village in the countryside. It is full of small farms and elderly retired people who have lived their whole lives in this small village.

Bourges is the principal town in the region of France known as *le Berry*. It is a town of about 90,000 residents with a large number of beautifully restored middle age buildings *en colombage*. This cathedral, along with Chartres, Reims and Amiens, is a world heritage site and is magnificent to see. However, it does not take long for us to figure out that the real reason for this excursion is not art and history. It is lunch at Le Cygne Restaurant. There are three fish courses, a meat course, cheese *bien sur*, dessert, wine and coffee. Here is the menu:

Ecrin de fruits de mer
Saumon au beurre d'oseille
Filet mignon, sauce Normande
Haricots verts et Pommes Noisettes
Trio de fromages sur lit de salads
Craquotant au Praliné et sa crème Anglaise
1/4 Vin
Café

We are about forty people on the bus and the average age is about seventy-five. Everyone can walk but many can't climb steps. Those who do walk are a little stiff in the knees and walk with a side-to-side motion. We look like a herd of geese wobbling along and Aprille assumes the role of a shepherd by helping the less agile to keep up. Movement is so difficult that I wonder why these trips are so popular, but then I remember dancing with these same *campagnards* at four o'clock in the morning just a few months ago. Senior citizens live well in France. They eat, drink and make merry every day. This spirit begins to show itself again as we head back to the bus. After suffering two hours of art and culture, we are ready to eat and the noise level on the bus rises as everyone becomes more animated. This is the *raison d'être*.

The excitement was a little too much for one lady who passed out at the dinner table. Another lady was slapping her so hard, she may have developed a concussion from the revival attempt. I guess they wanted to give her one last chance to eat but she never regained consciousness and was hauled off to the hospital. The most remarkable thing about this event was the reaction of all the other people. Except for a glance over the shoulder, everyone continued with their aperitifs and conversation. Only the tour operator and the restaurant owner seemed concerned. This army was not to be stopped by the wounded.

Aprille and I found a seat in the corner and were trying to get the P'tit Jules to join us but he disappeared into the bar and arrived too late. A large, elderly couple that we had not met before took the seats that we were saving. The lady seemed to have trouble understanding our French but her husband interpreted for us by yelling our words very loud. When the gentleman poured our wine, he told Aprille that wine was good for making the breast larger. His wife demonstrated by cupping her breast and lifting to show the result. Since she was at least seventy-five years old and larger than I, this was hardly coquette, but her husband seemed very pleased. I was beginning to understand why the others sitting at the table seemed so displeased with our tablemates.

When the waiter arrived with the first course, everyone started eating with the wrong fork. The first course was a seafood pastry that should be eaten with the fish fork and knife. Everyone was using the larger meat fork and knife. When the waiter returned he was thoroughly disgusted and looking up in exasperation. Some of the people discerned their mistake and tried to put the clean fish fork on the plate. This made matters worse because today we are having two fish courses and are supposed the keep the fish utensils for the second course. By the time the second fish course arrives the knives and forks of every description are everywhere. To make matters worse everyone is balling up their napkins and putting them on the table where the plate was just taken away. The waiter is pushing napkins out of the way, straightening the array of forks and scolding everybody's grandmother for their table manners. Bourges is not Paris but this waiter is taking on the airs of the big city. He is doomed to frustration because absolutely no one is paying any attention to him.

By the time we get to the filet mignon, those troublesome fish forks and knives have been taken away and everyone can concentrate on the food again. A plateau of filet mignon, green beans, tomatoes *provençal*, and potatoes is placed between each group of four people for self-service. As I try to present the plateau to the lady next to me, her husband protests a little and suggests that I serve Aprille first. I say no and continue to present the plateau to the lady. She takes close to half the meat, potatoes and green beans before her husband says "arrêt, ça c'est pour 4 personnes." She does everything but growl before conceding. Fortunately the other half is plenty for the remaining three people. In fact, I have eaten so much that I can't eat the three wedges of cheese that are served next. I take a taste of one and it is excellent but I leave the other pieces on the plate. Suddenly, I feel that eerie sensation of someone staring at me. I look over at the empty plate of my neighbor who has finished her cheese and see that she is staring at mine. Her husband senses the tension and gives her some of his Camembert.

The spoon at the top of the plate is for the dessert and since everything else has been taken away, everyone is back in step and the waiter is happy. The happiness is short lived. When he asks who would like coffee, someone asks if it is included in the price of the meal. He gets huffy again and snidely says yes and you can have a double coffee if you wish. This waiter is easily upset but again no one seems to notice his frustration. Actually, I suspect that everyone notices his frustration but this is French cinema and the scene is played out like this every day. The waiter is surly but his French customers ignore him because he is a servant. Even though these good country folk may not know all the complex rules of the table, they know how to handle a waiter.

The Source of the Loir

The hiking trail that traces the valley of the Loir River comes through my village of Lavardin. I have often wondered where the trail went in the up river direction. For some reason the trail down river is less interesting to me. My fascination with the idea of walking upstream to find the source of a river or stream started after I watched a documentary on public television about nineteenth century explorers trying to find the source of the Nile River in Africa. The various geographic societies in England and Europe were sponsoring expeditions to Africa in order to be the first to find the source of the Nile. These expeditions took months and sometimes years. Many of the explorers died or were crippled with the exotic diseases that they encountered. The explorer that I remember most clearly was Sir Richard Burton who went back time and again in this quest, only to die before one of his lieutenants finally made a disputed discovery. Eventually, an American journalist named Stanley got into the race and made an incredible expedition in which nearly everyone in his party died. But it was Stanley who finally reached Lake Tanganyika where he met a Scottish doctor named Livingston who had been living there for over thirty years. It was there that Stanley found fame and will always be remembered for the question "Dr. Livingston, I presume"?

The trek to the source of the Loir is less dramatic but at one time a young boy thought it was just as adventurous as the discovery of the Nile. Here is what Marcel Proust wrote about the source of the Loir:

> Never, in the course of our walks along the "Guermantes way," were we able to penetrate as far as the source of the [Loir], of which I had often thought and which had in my mind so abstract, so ideal an existence that I had been as surprised when someone told me that it was actually to be found in the same department, at a given number of miles from Combray, as I had been when I learned that there was another fixed point somewhere on the earth's surface, where, according to the ancients, **opened the jaws of Hell.**

Saint-Eman is a small commune of homes surrounding an eleventh century church and a spring fed *lavoir.* The women who washed cloths at this *lavoir* probably never considered it the jaws of Hell, but it is indeed the symbolic source of the Loir. I say "symbolic" because, like the Nile, there is a dispute as to the actual source. In the Jura Mountains I found several sources of rivers that came gushing out of the ground or the side of a mountain. I pictured something similar for the source of the Loir but it turns out to be a little more subdued. Many people believe the actual source is a series of lakes fifteen kilometers north of Saint-Eman near the village of Thieulin.

Four hundred years ago, a monastery owned these lakes and monks who lived in the monastery stocked them with trout. At that time there was a continuous stream from the overflow of those lakes to Lake

Villebon. The way the story goes is that there was a flood that covered the whole area and the trout that the monks were cultivating in the lakes swam into nearby Lake Villebon. This was devastating to the monks who lived in the winter off these trout. So facing starvation they went to the Lord of the manor who owned Lake Villebon and asked him if they could have their trout back. The Lord was the *duc de Sully* who was a minister of Henry IV and a leader in the religious reformation movement. The Lord, being a clever politician and in the opposite religious camp, told the monks that any trout that they could find wearing a monk's frock, they could keep as their own but all the others were his. The French have always had a good sense of humor. But the monks didn't think it was funny and retaliated by plugging up the source of their lake and forcing it to take the underground route to Saint-Eman.

The actual source of the Loir is probably a small valley just south of the forest of Champrond from which a small stream feeds Lake Villebon. The overflow from Lake Villebon and drainage from the plateau above Thieulin are probably the source of the spring-fed *lavoir* at Saint-Eman. Since the Loir only becomes recognizable as a river after leaving Saint-Eman and heading toward Illiers-Combray, the *lavoir* is probably the best testament to the source.

Perhaps Marcel Proust had the best idea about the source of the Loir. Just leave it to your imagination. For him it was always the open jaws of Hell.

Escargot

Escargot can be found all year around but June is the high season. I first noticed the abundance of snails in the month of June one morning as I walked to my mailbox to check the mail. With every step, I felt and heard a crunching sound under my feet. As I walked back to our cave home, I noticed something that looked like broken eggs all over the path. There were crushed shells and something that looked like egg yokes on the ground. I looked closer and discovered that they were snails that I had crushed on my way to the mailbox. I seem to have found one with every step. The rest were scurrying like…snails to get out of the way. I collected the rest to clear the path and perhaps enjoy at dinner. I soon learned that snails are something that you can gather for dinner but it will have to be dinner next month.

Escargot is not something that you pop in a pot of boiling water like shrimp or crabs. The process from garden to dinner table takes about three weeks. After gathering the snails you put them in a box to *maigrir* (lose weight) for a couple of weeks. Then they are washed and cleaned a number of times before they are ready for butter, garlic, etc. and the oven. Below is the recipe for *Escargots Moulin de Beaumé*.

Snails and shells can be purchased at almost any supermarket today but the thing that makes *Escargots Moulin de Beaumé* special is that Pierre and Claude Chêne gather and prepare the snails from their backyard. Only a handful of people still take the time to gather and clean snails.

When Christine Montambaux, la Dame de Villavard, told me she was gathering snails, I asked if I could watch her clean and prepare them. She found over a hundred on one day, which gave her a total of 214 so she called me to set a date. As usual, the event turned into a party but I got to see the whole process between aperitifs and dinner.

All 214 snails were put in a bucket of salt water and covered for about forty-five minutes. Most of the snails died in this process and began to *bave* (foam). Christine went through the process of washing and rinsing the snails at least eight times. Each time the cleaning process left old slimy water, which was dumped, on the flowers. After pouring out the last bucket of water, the snails were placed in a pan and covered with salt. They immediately began to *bave* again. Green slime reminiscent of a bad winter cold formed over the snails after about forty minutes. Christine washed and rinsed the snails again and then went through the whole salting process one more time.

After thoroughly washing and rinsing the snails one last time, she put the snails in a cooking pot with water, onions, cloves, bay leaves and thyme. The snails cooked for about forty-five minutes then were allowed to cool. Afterwards, she picked each snail from its shell and removed its intestines. *Et voila*. That is all there is to it. Just follow the recipe below that Claude Chêne gave me.

Escargots Moulin de Beaumé

For 50 escargots:
Ingredients for the beurre d'escargots:

250 grams of butter
15 grams of shallots
15 grams of parsley
10 grams of garlic
Pepper, salt, spices
6 filets of anchovies
1 centiliter of Pastis
    Mix the above ingredients all to together to make the beurre d'escargots.
A little white wine
50 grams of bread crumbs
Directions:
1. Put a little of the beurre d'escargots at the bottom of each shell.
2. Then put a snail in the shell.
3. Then close the shell with the same beurre d'escargots by compressing tightly.
4. Arrange the escargot on a platter and soak each one with a little white wine.
5. Sprinkle the butter with fine bread crumbs and put in the ovens on high for 8 minutes at the maximum.

Walnut Wine

The walnut tree has always been viewed with suspicion in the countryside of France. Many believe that sleeping in the shade of the walnut tree can cause a malady of the lungs that often kills. There is also a belief that lightening is most likely to strike the walnut tree and no one should stand under a walnut tree in a thunderstorm.

The walnut itself bears a completely different reputation. It is used in salads, sauces and all forms of cuisines. During the month of July, the nuts are harvested in the Loir Valley to make a special treat. It is an aperitif called *vin de noix* and is very easy to make.

Vin de Noix

Ingredients:
5 liters of red wine (9 pints)
1 liter of eau-de-vie (1 3/4 pints)
24 wet walnuts, quartered and pounded

1 kilogram of sugar (2 to 2 1/2 pounds)
1 vanilla pod
1 nutmeg, grated
6 cloves
(Wet walnuts are the mature green nuts, freshly picked from the tree)
Directions:
   Cut the nuts in quarters. Put the nuts, wine, eau-de-vie, sugar and spices into a large ceramic pot. Cover loosely and leave the mixture to macerate for 40 days. Strain the mixture through a double layer of dampened muslin, pour it into bottles and cork them carefully. Store in a cool place.

Feu de Saint Jean

Every year around 21 June our village celebrates the *feu de Saint Jean*. Although a religious meaning has been attached to this festival, it is in essence purely pagan. It is a celebration of the summer solstice and a ritual act of purification for the beginning of a new season. The ritual is to jump over the coals after the flames have subsided. Tort reform has revived this tradition but it is still mostly honored symbolically.

The church found it a convenient festival to adapt to its own use and decided to celebrate the birth of Saint John the Baptist on this day. It is from this date that the days become shorter up until 25 December. With the birth of Christ, the days become longer and, symbolically, the way of light begins.

Some villages build small symbolic fires but our village stacks logs about twenty feet high. The fire burns for several days but the real fun is the lighting ceremony and the trance-like state that follows as everyone quietly sits around watching it burn.

Relais d'Antan

When a Michelin starred chef calls you a *gourmand*, should you be flattered? When Aprille and I bought a copy of Paul van Gessel's book, **La Cuisine au Naturel**, he signed it with the comment, *Amitiés Gourmands*. Most English dictionaries define gourmand as someone who is gluttonous or greedy and who eats excessively. But French dictionaries define the term as someone who likes to eat good things. Since we often eat at Chef Gessel's Relais d'Antan restaurant in Lavardin, I assume he means that we are people who like to eat well. Certainly everyone who eats at the Relais d'Antan eats well because Paul has worked under the stars for many years. He was *chef de partie* of the three star Michelin restaurant Charles Barrier in Tours, which is an impressive accomplishment. Even more impressive is the two stars that he obtained for the Petit Nice restaurant in Marseilles in

1979 and the one star that he obtained for the La Couronne restaurant in Paris in 1985. He decided to open his own restaurant here in Lavardin in order to lead a less stressful life. Life along the Loir River is generally relaxed but I am not sure a French restaurant would ever be easy.

I asked Paul for one of his stress-less recipes to translate and prepare. It is a little more complicated than spinning a large haunch of meat from a string in front of a fireplace but well worth the effort. There are three white wines of the Loire Valley that go well with this dish, Sancerre, Quincy and Mennetou-Salon. Sancerre is relatively easy to find in the States but the other two are small regions in the Loire Valley that are rarely exported. Suffer with the Sancerre and bon appétit.

La Cuisine au Naturel
Par Paul Van Gessel
Le Relais d'Antan
Lavardin, France

Lobster Lasagna in a chive cream sauce

Ingredients for 6 people:
2 kilograms of Lobsters
200 grams of pasta noodles
1 kilogram of leeks
1 bunch of chives
100g of grated gruyere(Swiss) cheese
cumin (caraway)
Ingredients for pasta noodles:
200 grams of flour
2 eggs
Ingredients for the lobster sauce:
2 carrots
1 onion

1 shallot
1 branch of thyme
2 tomatoes
3 branches of tarragon
2 bulbs of garlic
8 branches of parsley
Cayenne pepper
3 grams of salt
1/2 liter of cream
1 deciliter of a dry white wine

Directions for lobster and leeks:

Peel and sauté the lobster tails in butter. Set aside the heads, legs and shells of the lobster for future use. Cut the white parts of the leeks in quarters, then wash and cut them in cubes. Put them in a bowl and season with salt and cumin. Add and pat of butter and a little water. Cover with saran wrap plastic and cook for 4 minutes 30 seconds in a microwave oven.

Directions for pasta noodles:

Put the flour in a bowl and add the eggs one by one while mixing thoroughly. Allow the dough to rest in the refrigerator for one hour. Roll the dough very thin and cook in salty water for 7 or 8 minutes. Drain and cut the pasta in pieces 8 centimeters by 5 centimeters.

Directions for the lobster sauce:

Crush the heads, legs and shell of the lobsters. Cut the carrots, onions and shallots into small cubes. Crush the tomatoes, garlic, tarragon and parsley. Put the carrots, onions, shallots, some thyme and rock salt in peanut oil. Add the crushed lobster parts and cook for 2 minutes together. Moisten it with 1 deciliter of dry white wine and for 2 minutes in order to evaporate the acidity of the wine. Add the cream then the crushed tomatoes, garlic, tarragon and Cayenne pepper. Bring it to a boil and allow it to cook for 2 minutes, and then let it soak for 1/2 hour. Strain it through a strainer and check for seasoning. In a soup bowl, put a layer of leeks, a layer of noodle, another layer of leeks, then the lobster tails. Sprinkle with half of the cheese. Brown lightly. Cover with the *rest of the noodles, then the rest of the cheese. Brown again. Pour the lobster sauce to which you have already added the chopped chives.*

Driving in France

Despite the best efforts of Rousseau and Voltaire, they missed the two most important rights of man in their writing. The first is that every Frenchman has the right to go as fast as he wants in his automobile. The second is that every Frenchman is entitled to a free unimpeded right-of-way while exercising the first right. These rights are not recorded anywhere but they are sacred nonetheless.

I first became aware of these unwritten rules while driving on the autoroutes of France. The posted speed limits are merely guidelines and not laws. Big trucks generally stay in the right hand lane and obey the posted limits but everyone else is testing the sound barrier. Speeds in excess of a 100 MPH are common in the far left lane where the timid never venture. A tiny speck in the rearview mirror can be on top of you in a matter of seconds. Little French cars tailgating at 90 MPH unnerve my friends from the States who ship their Porches over to enjoy the freedom of speed.

Despite this devotion to speed, the French, who are the most aggressive drivers in the world, become very cautious when entering the highway. They will do everything possible to avoid impeding the speed of the cars already on the road. It is not because they are courteous. It is because right-of-way is an essential element of speed. The French revere both these rights but the subject of right-of-way is much more complex.

In the nearby village of Les Roches, a truck slammed into the seven hundred year-old church while passing through the village. The village sued for damages but the court ruled in favor of the trucking company stating that it didn't matter that the church had been there for seven hundred years, it should not have been in the right-of-way of the truck.

I notice this phenomena everyday as I chug along in my diesel Mercedes at incredibly slow speeds of 75 MPH and less. Little French cars are always attached to my rear bumper trying to catch a draft and slingshot around my lumbering beast. And why not? Dragging along behind me for two blocks to the supermarket might cost them fifteen seconds of their life.

Passing the car in front is the most important part of a French driver's life. My friend Fai has been trying to get his French drivers license for over a year. He drove for years in New York City while working for the Treasury Department but he was not prepared for the French boot camp called driving school. His instructor shows nothing but contempt for Fai's refusal to go faster that 80 MPH. Fai explains that such speeds on narrow, winding country roads with no shoulders is too dangerous. He says that eighty percent of the course is concerned with overtaking and passing the car in front.

The written part of the test is even harder and is full of trick questions. For example: When approaching a pedestrian-crossing with a pedestrian standing at the curb, do you stop and yield to the pedestrian? Fai answered yes. The answer is no. The instructor explained that since the pedestrian has not shown any intent to enter the crossing, he is fair game. If he has a foot in the lane, then you must stop because the advancing foot shows intent. Another example: If you are following a vehicle going the speed limit, do you have the right to pass it? The answer is yes, always.

The exam is reputed to be full of such trick questions but Fai never got a chance to take the test. Instead of giving him the actual address of the place of examination, his instructor insisted that he follow him in his car. At the first tollbooth, the instructor sped off and was never seen again. Fai decided not to signup for the test again after he learned that the supposedly non-Francophone test was is French.

Those who actually graduate from driving school have to display a large red Hawthornian A in the rear window of their car for one year. The large red A means that the driver is a trained killer and is on probation for the year. I have learned to keep my distance from the big red A's. They are either pissed off about the A or inspired from the course but they are the most aggressive drivers on the road.

Many people elect not to drive in France. Aprille, who loves to drive in New York City, refuses to drive here. I have met many other people who have made the same decision. The French have the highest death rate in the world. The local newspaper has daily articles about single car accidents where all of the occupants are carbonized from the ensuing fire. These cars go so fast that fires are common when they crash.

Those drivers who aren't carbonized are usually crippled for life. The government recognizes this problem and has setup rehabilitation centers around France. There is one just across the river in Montoire. As summer approaches the streets are full of these paraplegics motoring around in exotically outfitted wheelchairs that they steer by blowing in a tube. I once saw a man who could not sit in a chair in a motorized bed driving around in downtown Montoire. It is a great program for people who would otherwise have no life but life on the motorways of France is always risky.

Last summer a paraplegic in a motorized wheelchair was struck by a speeding car in our village and knocked over. The collision caused his life support tubes to become disconnected and he died. I never saw anything about this incident in the newspaper. I suspect the driver was never punished. After all, he has the right to drive as fast as he wants and is entitled to a clear right of way to do so.

The Finger

I normally park in the chateau parking lot but today the car was full of things to take up the hill so I parked on the street. After parking, I saw one of those little French cars in the rearview mirror coming at the usual speed of 90 MPH. He came screeching to a halt behind me before realizing that I was parked. I guess he was a little embarrassed so he gave me the finger, American style. Of course in the States this is an invitation to pull out your Glock and empty eighteen rounds into the radiator but I don't think this vulgar gesture means the same thing to the French. Ironically, giving the finger originated in France but it was the English who invented it. Here is a brief history that my friend, Kent Dykes, sent me on the subject:

A Little history lesson for you... History of Giving the Finger: Should be in everyone's Book of Knowledge!

```
>                        _
>                      /'_/)
>                     /_ /
>        /           / /
>          /'_'/'  '/'__'7,
>         /'/  /  /  /" /_\
>        ('(  '  '    _~/' ')
>        \          '   /
>        '\' \       _.7'
>          \         (
>          \          \
Giving the Finger
```

Before the Battle of Agincourt in 1415, the French, anticipating victory over the English, proposed to cut off the middle finger of all captured

English soldiers. Without the middle finger it would be impossible to draw the renowned English longbow and therefore be incapable of fighting in the future.

This famous weapon was made of the native English Yew tree, and the act of drawing the longbow was known as "plucking the yew" (or "pluck yew").

Much to the bewilderment of the French, the English won a major upset and began mocking the French by waving their middle fingers at the defeated French, saying, "See, we can still pluck yew! PLUCK YEW!"

Since 'pluck yew' is rather difficult to say, the difficult consonant cluster at the beginning has gradually changed to a labiodental fricative 'F', and thus the words often used in conjunction with the one-finger-salute are mistakenly thought to have something to do with an intimate encounter. It is also because of the pheasant feathers on the arrows used with the longbow that the symbolic gesture is known as "giving the bird".

I can't top this story but I have to add one thing that demonstrates the continuing rivalry between the French and the English. I visited Azincourt with my friend Greg Bennett who has a vacation home nearby. There is nothing to see except the battlefield that looks like thousands of other fields in France. However, on the anniversary of this battle a horde of English types cross the channel to celebrate this six hundred year-old victory. They get drunk while marching around singing and giving the finger. The French seem mildly amused at this behavior. What can you expect from *les rosbifs*?

La Résistance

As the rain taps on my hood, I can hardly believe what I am seeing from my perch on the bridge. I watch a short muscular man moving through the shallows of the river setting charges and running wires. He moves like a seal through the dark cold waters of the Loir River. Again and again, he crosses the river to set a charge and run a wire. He appears to be ready to blow this twelfth century bridge. He has the cold hard stare of a veteran. Some say he can open an oyster with that look but it is the firm jaw that shows his determination. The people here call him Coco but his real name is Olivier Tremblay and he has been the explosives expert for the village for longer than anyone cares to remember. I have known Coco for years but Kiki, his assistant, is a new man in town and no one knows if he can be trusted. To make matters worse, another man has been recruited who may or may not be on our side. The explosives team calls him Titi.

As Kiki attaches the last wire to the plunger, a fleet of six dragon shaped vessels appear around the bend in the river. It is too late to run now. Either the plan works or we run to the caves on the hill. As the attackers approach, the plunger is pushed and an explosion of fire and thunder turns the river red. Out of the corner of my eye, I see blood red flames glowing from the thick acrid smoke billowing from the chateau high on the mountain. We have been tricked. The chateau is under attack. The river attack is just a diversion.

When the fireworks are over, I ask who is responsible for this great show. I am told that Coco and Didi handled the fireworks and the music. I know Coco and Kiki, and I met Titi for the first time tonight. But who the hell is Didi? It must be a code name for Stephen Spielberg because no local could have produce this kind of spectacle. But I am wrong. It turns out Coco is the main producer of the fireworks and has been doing it for years. It is the best sound and light show that I have seen and well worth the wait until midnight to see it. But I am not the only one to wait. Hundreds of people make the effort to come here every year to see the show and eat *moules frites. Vive la Résistance.*

Independence Day is celebrated on the fourteenth of July in France. Americans call it Bastille Day. In Lavardin, we celebrate it on the night of the thirteenth and the early morning hours of the fourteenth. There are fireworks and a sound and light show on the river. Aprille and I volunteered to help with the celebration this year but our contribution is small compared to other people of the village who work on this festival all year long. The first meeting was back in May and everything seemed well organized until the subject of food came up. The complicated sound and light show was passed off to the experts, but everyone had a different idea and suggestion to make about the food. What, no Camembert? Are you kidding, no mergeuz? You are going to serve food on plastic plates? Plastic glasses for the wine? *Quel horreur! Dégueulasse!* We spent an hour debating the food problem and finally agreed to meet again in June. I agreed to work all day on the twelfth and thirteenth setting up the tables, chairs and tents. Aprille volunteered too, but everyone agreed that this was a man's job and that she should show up for the *moules* cleaning and the decoration committee. Actually cleaning the *moules* turns out to be a huge job and takes fifteen to twenty people all day long to clean enough for the five or six hundred people expected.

Jean-Claude Aubert and Jean Mahoudeau build and assemble the Viking ships that descend the Loir. Gerard Verger assembles the band-stand and dance floor. Pierre Chavigny, our recently retired mayor, cooks the *moules*. Charles Brousset manages the *buvette*. Nicole Norguet cooks the fries. Another group cooks the sausages and the new mayor, Gerard Allaire, works around the clock and does a little of everything.

Recipe for Mussels
Put about 1/2 Kilo of mussels for each person in large pot with a very dry white wine, fresh cream, onions, garlic, shallots, parsley, bay laurel and thyme. Simmer until all the shells are open. Serve in the soup.

Système D

I report for duty on the morning of the twelfth to help set up the steel-framed tents. The mayor, Gerard Allaire, asks me to help the team of about ten men who are hooking long steel bars together to make a frame for the tents. These tents will shelter our guests from the rain. As I approach the team, I see a steel bar arcing toward my head and I duck down and to the right. Another bar comes arcing from the left and I stretch back, down and to the left. I feel like Kenu Reeves dodging bullets on the rooftop in *Matrix* but I quickly adapt to the rhythm of the swinging steel.

Most of these men are in their mid-sixties, so the pace slows down as the work progresses and comes to a near stop when the task involves bending all the way down to the ground to pickup something. It will take two

full days to set up the tents, tables and chairs and one full day to disman-
tle everything afterwards. The occasion is Lavardin's annual Independence
Day celebration and the whole village participates.

Work starts at eight o'clock in the morning but in France everyone
stops for a two-hour lunch break and a periodic bottle of wine. At our first
break, everyone stands around looking at a bottle in embarrassed silence.
No one has a corkscrew. It is as if we have all been emasculated. There is a
lot of mumbling and I hear the occasional *merde, quelle horreur* or *et alors*
before Gerard Verger, the village *menusier* (skilled carpenter), pulls out a
large screw and drills it into the cork with his portable drill. He then takes
a nail-puller from his tool belt and uncorks the bottle by pulling on the
screw head.

This clever solution is what the French call *système D*. The 'D' stands
for the French word *débrouiller* that means to solve or work out a problem
in a clever, inventive way. The people in the countryside seem particularly
adept at these solutions but it is also a national characteristic. The phrase,
système D, can be found in every French dictionary. It is very much like
what we call American ingenuity.

When I read in Polly Platt's book, *French or Foe*, that the French are
Cartesian and prefer to live by logic and systems, I found this concept
hard to accept. To me everything seemed to run on *système D* with very little logic involved. But after living in France for some years, I am beginning to see that there are systems here that are based on logic. Perhaps they
should be called *système B* for the word *brouiller* which means to mix up or
confuse something. An example might be Charles de Gaulle Airport or the
system of yielding to the right of way instead of putting up traffic signs at
every intersection. On the other hand, *rond-points* (traffic circles) work
beautifully.

As one of my neighbors said to me after watching the cork pop out of
the bottle with a Phillips head screw in it, "*c'est fou, mais ça marche quand
même.*" It's crazy but it works nevertheless. I have been collecting unusual

corkscrews for a wall decoration but I am now replacing them all with my Black and Decker drill, a screw and my Stanely pliers.

Les Manouches

In the old John Wayne western movies, there was always a good pilgrim in the wagon train who thought that he could make peace with the Indians. When the wagons were circled against attacking Indians, he would invariably sneak off at night to show the savages that they were god fearing Christians who only wanted to live in peace. The next morning they would find him skinned alive and staked to an anthill.

I think of these old movies every time I see a caravan of gypsies parked in the *terrain de voyageurs*. These people seem to be completely unapproachable, which makes them that much more mysterious. They have been traveling the roads of Europe for hundreds of years and their culture remains basically unchanged. They travel in small tribes or families and never seem to stay in one place for a long time. Some still pull their old style wagons with horses like in the Dracula movies, but most now travel in modern RVs.

Our first contact with the gypsies was in front of the local supermarket where the women sell baskets. Aprille has a penchant for baskets and wanted to buy one. Her real motivation was to help the poor gypsies feed their children. But my friends have warned me to avoid them and I noticed that the French were circling them like a pit of rattlesnakes. Aprille, however, who is a little left of Lennon politically, decides that if we show them that we love them, we can get a good deal on a basket and feed a child.

It does not take much to get them started. I make eye contact and four women rise like flies from a pile of garbage. They are literally buzzing with offers and deals. One woman holding up three baskets is yelling *cent francs* (fifteen dollars) and I am thinking that fifteen dollars for three baskets is really a good deal. I make the deal and hand her a hundred franc note but she doesn't let go of the baskets. My hundred franc note has disappeared and she now says the price is two hundred francs.

We are pulling back and forth on the basket and I realize that a crowd is gathering to watch the spectacle. This is where the old axiom "If you are stupid, you will pay for it everyday of your life" comes from. I say okay and pull out a two hundred franc note thinking that I will get my hundred franc note back as change. The two hundred franc note disappears and she is still gripping the baskets. The price has gone up to four hundred francs but she is throwing in another small basket as a *cadeau*. While all this is going on, the other three women are jabbering away and sticking baskets in my face. By the time we walk away, we have enough baskets to open a boutique and they only cost us about a hundred dollars. Aprille is happy but I feel like I have been skinned alive.

Aprille was content with the transaction because she was more of an observer and did not get involved in the basket tug of war and the magic spells cast by these women. When my good little pilgrim later tried to approach the basket vendors alone she came away with a completely different point of view. She still loves their baskets but would never try to buy one again.

Aprille learned from her experience but I will from time to time get sucked in again. Aside from magic spells, it is the tactic of holding up a beautiful basket and saying "ten francs" that occasionally gets me. Another old maxim is that people tend to make the same mistakes over and over again. I have on two other occasions since my ordeal handed over ten francs without thinking. At least I have learned to abandon the ten francs and walk away. One has to pay for it everyday.

The French are remarkably tolerant of the gypsies. There are special rules that allow them to get around compliance with social welfare and compulsory education standards for their children. I don't know what the government does about taxes but I suspect that they don't bother trying to collect them. The gendarmes watch them closely and usually visit their camps to recover stolen items as soon as they are reported missing. The locals grumble about the lack of punishment for their thievery but seem to accept it as a fact of life. They are notorious for taking anything not nailed down. That is the reason every French home has a fence and a garage that are locked every night. I think that the gypsies are tolerated because they are not violent. They are master thieves but they do it quietly at night with surreptitious magic. No one has ever caught a gypsy in the act of stealing. Only the circumstantial evidence of chairs, tables, cloth's lines and license plates found in their camps suggest their guilt.

The gypsies are still a mystery to me. The unknown places they come from and go to after they leave add to the romantic notions of their travels. There must be something in this lifestyle that is appealing enough to sustain it for so long. The local libraries are full of books about local and national traditions but there is very little to be found about the gypsies. It is because they are unapproachable and I like that.

The Accident

Aprille had an accident. She hit a car parked on the road in the village. I walked down the hill and left a note on the car with my telephone number. The eighty-year-old couple who own the car called the next morning and said to come down and talk about it. Monsieur and Madame Beaujouan own the house on the corner of the town square and sell bottles of propane gas to supplement their income. I had met them before when I bought gas and one other occasion when Monsieur Beaujouan invited us to have a drink in his cave under the chateau. He had introduced himself as Beaujouan *le lapin*. Lapin is the word for rabbit and this good-natured man was joking about the speed that he does not move at. But having one drink with a Frenchman is more like a handshake than a bonding event. You have to drink daily to truly bond. The point is that I don't know Monsieur and Madame Beaujouan very well so I bring all of my insurance and registration papers just in case I have to buy a new car.

I am greeted at the door by two smiling faces who invite me in and offer me a seat. Of course we start the meeting with a *petit verre*. It is eleven o'clock in the morning so we are close enough to the lunch hour to start with an aperitif. Otherwise it would have been a breakfast digestif. We spend about a half hour sipping Madame Beaujouan's *feuille de pêcher*, which she is rightly proud of.

As we approach the lunch hour, we quickly get down to business and agree to meet again tomorrow to discuss the accident further.

The following morning I meet Monsieur Beaujouan and we drive over to the garage of Jean-Marie Cabart who is also a resident of Lavardin and a relative of our new mayor. There is more damage than first appeared, so Jean Marie calls my insurance agency and arranges a meeting so we can do the paperwork. Our friend Monique Petit-Brazier handles the paperwork at the agency of Gilles Proust where I have my insurance. Monique's brother is a winemaker in the village of Thoré-La-Rochette where she also lives. Monique tells me that it was her parents who invented the *pousse d'épine* aperitif that is similar to Madame Beaujouan's *feuille de pêcher*.

After finishing the claim forms, we head back to the Beaujouan homestead where I am given a tour of the garden and an offer of a glass of wine from the Beaujouan cave under the chateau. I know that one cannot conclude a car accident claim without a drink even if it is ten o'clock in the morning. We head up National 10, which is the name that he calls the cement path running through the middle of his garden, and arrive at his cave under the chateau. The cave is actually a part of the old underground system of tunnels that run for miles under the chateau.

On the way to the cave we meet Charles Brousset who is on his way to open the chateau boutique where you can always find a glass of wine if you get caught with a thirst between home and the next cave. Monsieur Beaujouan invites Charles to join us in the large, well-stocked cave. There is a huge boulder in the ceiling just at the entrance of the cave that looks as if it is ready to fall. Charles expresses his concern but *Le Lapin* just laughs and says that it has been there for a thousand years. Just in case, Charles and I stand back from the line of fire.

Monsieur Beaujouan asks if we want white or red? I answer "Red."

"Bordeaux, Burgundy or Chinon?" I say, "Chinon."

"Old or new?" Charles answers, "Good".

After two large glasses, Monsieur Beaujouan says that you can't put a cork back in a bottle of red. It will spoil. We agree and finish the bottle. Charles invites us over for another *petit verre* at the chateau boutique. After another glass of red, we head home for…. what does one do at half past ten in the morning after a couple bottles of wine? Wait for the next accident.

Feuille de Pêcher

Ingredients:

1 liter of eau-de-vie (made from the fruit on the trees in your garden).

5 liters of wine (rosé is preferred).

Leaves from your peach tree.

Sugar

Directions:

Mix it all together in a ceramic container and allow it to rest for six weeks. Strain, bottle and serve cold. Madam Beaujouan assures me that it is all natural and all of the products come from their large garden in the back of their house.

Liberation
11 August 1944

It was fifty-seven years ago when American jeeps and tanks rolled into Montoire-sur-Loir to liberate the village. There happened to be a reporter from Paris present on that occasion who took a photograph of a young girl handing an American soldier a bouquet of flowers. This old photograph reappears every year on the 11th of August when the village celebrates the day of liberation. My friend Jean Montambaux has been telling me about this celebration for weeks. Jean is seventy years old but was only twelve when he first saw American soldiers. Like most of the seventy-somethings of this region, Americans are remembered fondly. In stark contrast to the German invaders, the Americans brought chewing gum, chocolate and liberation. Everybody has a war story about the arrival of the Americans and a few even have old American Jeeps that are immaculately restored and maintained.

The ceremony starts at the old train station and I am a little surprised to see so many people present. Several hundred people have shown up to listen to speeches and march behind a cavalcade of jeeps and men dressed up in old GI uniforms carrying M-1 rifles. The mayor, the Counsel General of the region and other political figures make speeches and present awards to the U.S. Army captain who is present to assist in the celebration. A young girl, who is dressed up in a 1940's dress and coiffure, presents the Captain with a bouquet of flowers and everyone poses for photographs. There is an older lady standing beside the young girl who is introduced to me as Madame Martineau. Jean tells me that she was the young girl in the fifty-seven-year-old photograph.

There are so many people present that it is hard to get close enough to get a picture of the GIs but I spot one rugged looking individual who looks like his name ought to be Bubba. I ask if I can take his picture. He answers, "*oui, bien sur,*" and I see that he is my neighbor Gaston Cottenceau from Lavardin. Gaston has one of the old original Jeeps that looks brand new. Jean tells me that it is a Willis, which is the best. The Fords are okay but everybody here prizes the Willis Jeeps. He points out another Jeep that looks exactly like the others to me but Jean tells me that it is a modern knockoff and shakes his head disgust.

Jean and I stay for all of the events including the march to the *mairie* where crowds of people are engulfing the captain as if he just liberated the town again. I don't get a chance to talk to the captain but I am invited to celebrate the liberation at the caves of Pierre Capps and Monsieur Jean. At Jean's cave Marcel Rousselet tells me about watching a German soldier on the top of the chateau in Montoire shooting anybody who walked in the streets. He sniped from his perch all day until he ran out of ammunition. The Germans came looking for Marcel once and he hid in the hay in a barn until they gave up the search. Others were caught and hauled off to work in labor camps in Germany. Those young men never returned and no one knows what happened to them.

Jean said that the Germans would walk around shooting people as they were retreating. People had to hide from the retreating Germans but the Americans were just a few hours behind the retreating Army. People sometimes mistakenly ran cheering into the streets only to discover the approaching vehicles were Germans. Those who were present tell me the risk was worth the chance to see the Americans and get some chewing gum.

The Circus

The people of the Beauce have a reputation of being dour, crabby people who are too serious about working in their Kansas-like wheat fields. While hiking through this region, I decide to stop for lunch at a small restaurant in the village of Alluyes. I enter through the bar and see that the dining room is empty. The bar is full of men drinking beer and to my horror some are drinking water. My friends in the *bas vendômois* warned me that the Beaucerons might act like this. I ask the lady at the bar if the restaurant is open and she directs me to a seat at a long table where an older gentleman is sitting. She sits me directly in front of this man even though no one else is in the room.

There is an uncomfortable silence between this man and myself as we begin our meal. I try to make conversation but we have little to talk about. We finally agree that the food is *pas terrible mais copieux.*[5] At precisely one o'clock all of the men in the bar enter the dining room and take seats at

---

[5] The food is not very good but plentiful.

the table. This only multiplies the tension as dozens of blank faced, silent men stare at each other.

As the meal is being served a circus wagon full of lions and tigers stops in the square with music from the opera *Carmen* blasting on loud speakers. I want to get up and run outside to witness this unusual event but, other than glancing over the shoulder, no one else moves so I settle for a glimpse of the lions out of the window. I ask the older gentleman who I now consider my best friend if this happens all the time. He says, in monotone, that things like this never happen here. Maybe these people are as boring as I have been told.

By the time I leave the village, I am solidly hooked on the idea of seeing those lions and tigers. When I reach the village of Bonneval, I hear the music from *Carmen* again but I can't find the wagon with the lions and tigers. It turns out that the noise is coming from a small van with a loud speaker advertising the circus. Again, I have missed the lions and tigers. I find a poster that gives the time and place of the show. The first performance is today.

By the time I find the circus, the performance has already started inside an orange and blue tent but all the animals are parked outside. There are lions, an impressive Bengal tiger, a large black horse, a small brown pony, a large camel named Algie, and a gaggle of llamas.

The performers appear to be refugees from the Ed Sullivan Show. There is the guy on the ten-foot unicycle juggling flaming sticks and spinning hoops on his legs. There is the magician who throws colored scarves into a top hat then pulls them out all tied together with a couple of birds. There is also a comedian who tells jokes for the kids and two young acrobats who swing from ropes and balance themselves on chair legs. But the real stars are the horses, camels and llamas that run around the ring jumping a steel bar.

I am impressed with the group. It is called the Franck Zavatta Circus. The performers are young, attractive men and women who are at all times professional and polite. I am more accustomed to the county fairs in the States that were seedy operations run by toothless middle-aged men wearing tobacco stained T-shirts. The circuses of Europe also had a dubious reputation before the turn of the last century. The worst were the Romanian gypsies whose acts were little more than distractions to help the band steal chickens.

It was the Zavatta family that brought respect to the circus in Europe. When the daughter of an Italian count ran off with and married the circus performer Demetrio Zavatta, their children and the name Zavatta took on noble origins. But it was not noble blood that brought this troupe respect. It was a reputation for honesty and professionalism that earned the Zavatta Circus the mark of distinction. The famous clown Achille Zavatta was the youngest son of Demetrio and his older brother, Rodolphe, performed and managed the Cirque Zavatta in Europe for many years. Demetrio's father, Antonio Zavatta, was the first to use the *chapiteau* (movable tent) and developed the use of clowns in comedy routines.

Several times a year the fields along the Loir River fill up with grazing camels, llamas and water buffalo. I don't have to see a poster to know the circus has come to town. Now I know why older generations always dreamed of running away with circus. It is too bad these small circuses don't exist in America. There is now only a handful touring the countryside of France.

Confrérie des Chevaliers de la Puette et du Franc-Pinot Vallée du Loir

When Monsieur Jean asked me if I would like to join *La Confrérie de la Puette et du Franc-Pinot*, I hesitated to say yes. The problem with joining a group is that you become a part of what they officially stand for. I once joined a college fraternity, which was a great experience, but it was not until after I graduated that I first saw the fraternity charter. It was worse than an Alabama county club. I immediately realized that I would never be a Supreme Court Justice or high elected official. Also, there is the problem of the secrets. It was only after I learned the secret handshake that I was told that if I ever revealed it to a non-brother, a hawk would swoop down from the sky and pluck out my heart. I have learned to live comfortably with the idea of not being a Supreme Court Justice but that damn hawk haunts me everyday.

I know that *confréries* are wine drinking fraternities that today include women members. I have seen pictures of these distinguished looking men and women dressed in black velvet robes with large gold medals and exotic looking hats. They are truly impressive but I need more information. I don't even know what a *puette* is. Monsieur Jean arranges a meeting with Monsieur Yves Norguet who is a former Grand Master and the doyen of the winemakers in the Vendômois. Monsieur Norguet is a walking advertisement for the consumption of wine. At eighty-seven, his age is a mathematical formula in French, 4 x 20 +7 = 87, but his eyes belie his age. He sparkles like a *vin petillant*. He moves slowly and his hands shake a bit but he is delighted that I have asked for information on the history of the Confrérie. He asks Jean some questions that seem to surprise him. He tells me he never knows when Jean is serious or playing a joke on him. He evidently does it all the time. We agree that I will be *intronisé* (inducted) at the wine fair in Thoré-La-Rochette in August. He gives me some old newspaper articles and forms to fill out and orders us to follow him on a slow circuit to the Norguet *chai* where a glass of wine seals the deal.

When I learn that my friend Charles Brousset is being inducted into the *Confrérie* at the wine fair in Montoire during the Pentecost weekend, I decide to go to the ceremony to see what I am getting into. The black robed Immortals are lined up on the stage in somber fashion. Monsieur Norguet looks impressive in his black velvet robe but the group of inductees is impressive too. The candidates included the Mayor of Montoire, businessmen and some local winemakers. Yves conducts the ceremony and reads the rites of induction while tapping the new members on the shoulder with a huge, polished vine root. As he taps the shoulders he reads the oath:

> *Au nom de Bacchus et Saint Vincent,*
> *Pour la Glorification des vins*
> *De notre bonne Vallée du Loir,*
> *Blancs, gris, rouges et rosés fruités,*

Que tout un chacun se doit boire
Sois Chevalier de la Confrérie
De la Puette et du Franc-Pinot.

The first inductee is a small lady who listens to the oath and is handed a huge glass of wine filled to the rim. It is about a half-bottle of wine. She has to drink the whole glass without stopping while these noble looking men and women sing something akin to "drink chug-a-chug" to the tune of *Frère Jacques*. Since she is the first, she has to stand on the stage until the other seven people are inducted. Each is given this large glass of wine but no one else's glass is nearly as full as the first lady who immediately turns red as a beet. I am sure the stage must seem like a tightrope after the wine sets in but she manages to make it through the ceremony. Most people go straight home and go to bed after drinking so much but my friend, Charles, manages to stay on his feet and dance all night at the Winemaker's Dinner afterward. This is almost as impressive as the lady's performance.

I make another trip to the Norguet vineyard to get more information from Monsieur Norguet. He tells me that the original confrérie was La Confrérie du Pinot-Franc that was founded by Dr. René Henry in 1956 and that he was one of the original inductees. Here is the oath that he took:

Par le grand Virgile qui chanta la vigne,
par le grand Rabelais qui chanta le vin,
par le grand Ronsard qui chanta le Loir,
je vous sacre Chevalier du Franc-Pinot.

I also learn that Yves was instrumental in combining the Confrérie du Pinot-Franc with the Confrérie de la Puette in 1980. The *Confrérie de la Puette* was founded in 1946 and has its origins in the Sarthe region down river. A *puette* is a small piece of wood that plugs the hole at the bottom of a barrel of wine. The winemaker uses it to taste the progress of the *vinification*.

I read that Pinot-Franc was argot for the chenin grape but Monsieur Jean tells me that it is the *pineau d'aunis* grape. Jean is usually right.

The day of induction has arrived and I am getting a little nervous about the chug-a-lug part of the ceremony. This particular wine fair has always been popular and there are hundreds of people present as well as a number of distinguished government officials. What if I get sick on the stage? As I am waiting at the wine tasting area I see my friends Marc and Monique Petit-Brazilier. They offer me a glass but I say that I will wait until after the ceremony. Marc says that is a good idea because when he went through the ceremony he had to drink a whole bottle and got sick. Now, I am getting a little queasy. Monique tells me that her nephew, Benoit Brazilier, is also being inducted today. When I meet Benoit, he tells me of having to drink a whole liter of wine at another ceremony. I decide that I don't want to hear any more stories and go over to the stage where the ceremony will take place. While waiting, the crowd begins to grow and I spot some familiar faces. Monsieur Jean and the P'tit Jules are in the front row making faces and cracking jokes. They have never joined a confrérie and I begin to wonder why?

The stage fills with the black-robed officers of the confrérie and the visiting dignitaries. The crowd falls silent and the inductees are called to the stage one at the time. When my name is called I climb the first two steps, trip on the third and accept the assistance of the Grand Chambellan to find my place. I stand before the Grand Maitre as he reads my biography to the crowd. He concludes by stating the following:

You are a writer and a member of the association of Resurgence. You love our country, the valley of the Loir and its wines. You live here in one of the most beautiful villages of France, Lavardin. You appreciate the wines of the *Coteaux du Vendômois, du Jasnieres* and *du Coteaux du Loir*, but you are also a gourmet of Bordeaux, Chinon, Gamay de Touraine, Tavel and Muscadet, as well as, Quincy and Sancerre. In making you today at Thoré-La-Rochette, *Chevalier de la Puette and du Franc-Pinot*, our brotherhood knows that you will be in the United States a well-informed ambassador of our beautiful Valley of the Loir.

Next the *Grand Bailli* taps my shoulder with a polished vine root of the *cépage* Pinot-Franc while the *Grand Maitre* reads the following oath:

> *In the name of Bacchus and Saint Vincent,*
> *For the Glorification of the wines*
> *Of our good Valley of the Loir,*
> *White, rose, red and roses fruites,*
> *That everyone ought to drink,*
> *I make you Chevalier de la Confrérie*
> *De la Puette et du Franc-Pinot.*

A large sliver medal attached to a blue, white and red ribbon is draped around my neck by a pretty young girl who kisses me four times. After the last oath is read, each of the five inductees is given a large glass of wine equivalent to a half-bottle. It seems huge in my hand but it is much less that a liter. After a toast we are instructed to drink and the black robed figures begin to sing:

> *Buvez-vous, Buvez-vous,*
> *vos petits verres, vos petits verres,*
> *glugla, glugla, glugla, glugla....*

It is a very good *pineau d'aunis gris* and I drink it as fast as I can but I don't finish first. Benoit knows the technique of opening the throat and pours it down a good 10 seconds before me. The only lady in the group has some trouble finishing but finally manages it. We are given certificates and instructed by the *Grand Bailli* and the *Premier Echevin* to sign the *Livre d'Or*. The certificate says that I have suffered the test of the *entonnage* of the wines of the Valley of the Loir and have been found worthy to be a Chevalier. There are no secrets to keep. I search the sky and it is clear.

Provence Notes
Rosé Wine

When most people think of France they think of Paris or Provence. I have been to Paris many times but I prefer my cave in the Loir Valley to anything that Paris has to offer. But If I had to make a choice between my sweet little valley and Provence, then the decision would be much more difficult. Of course Provence offers so many obvious pleasures like its warm, dry sunny weather and beaches. Its mountains offer skiing within thirty minutes from the beach in winter. Like every region in France, it has amazing regional cuisine. It has *boules*, pastis and olive trees. It has chateaux, fortresses, grottos and the ancient remains of the Roman Empire. But for me, the quality that makes my loyalty waver when I think of Provence is its rosé wines.

We have rosé in the Touraine that is just as good, but it is markedly different. The rosés of our region are fruity tasting wines that reflect the *terroir* and personality of the Touraine. They are sweet and mild like life in our valley. The rosés of Provence also reflect the *terroir* and personality of their region. They are dry, edgy wines that taste of lavender, cedar and rosemary. Just breathing the air from the terrace of our room reminds me of *rosé*. There is a strong smell of lavender in the air, but it is much more complex than just one aroma. It is the smell of lavender with the accompanying scents of herbs, cedar and pine.

The rosé of Provence is also dry and clean like the air, which is fresh and carries sound clearly for great distances. I can see far across the ridges that finger down from the high Alps, and I can hear the details of life on the opposing hillside. I can hear a sweeping broom and a chair being moved at some distant domicile. These sounds belie the fact that they are coming from miles away and that we are separated by gorges hundreds of feet deep. It is like noises coming from the next room. This dry, warm air carries little sounds great distances, yet it is quiet enough to hear the few noises being made. But it is not the noise that impresses the senses. It is the tranquility and quietness surrounding the noise. As the sun begins to set, I hear one lone cicada starting its concert and it sounds like a symphony in the desert. This is Provence.

Provence Notes
All Good Things

The red tiled roofs of the vacation homes of the rich and famous paint the hillsides and cliff faces for the length of the *provençal* coast. Despite the crowds of foreigners who infect this ancient culture, Provence has a charm and ambiance like nowhere else in the world. It has a depth of history and culture that no tourist trap can destroy. I have been to Provence on a number of other occasions but those trips were more as a tourist passing through. This trip is definitely different. We will be here two weeks and we have a purpose. As you may have already guessed, I am using the royal we which means that Aprille has a purpose and I'm going along for the ride. But it is giving me an opportunity to learn a little more about the region.

We were invited to stay at the villa of our friends, Scott and Nancy McLucas. Although they are Americans, Scott has lived in Cagnes sur Mer for over thirty years and knows the area well. Nancy has lived here since their marriage ten years ago and is *passionée pour la vie française*, even more so than Scott. Scott and Nancy live in the States six months of the year but I sense that they would have no problem living here all year long.

It was by Scott's recommendation that Aprille was invited to show one of her sculptures at the Musée Renoir in Cagnes sur Mer. He is a member of the board of directors of the museum and participates in many of its projects. He works for a small foundation that helps promising artists and has commissioned work from Aprille in the past. Aprille and Scott have a passion for the arts and can talk for hours about things that few people can follow. I am not one of the few who can follow the conversations but that is no problem. Nancy and I have our own animated conversations but the subject is different. We talk about *la vie en rose*. All I have to do is bring up a topic about France like wine or food to get Nancy started. She is like a sunflower at noon. She stands up squarely and her face lifts like a soprano delivering her music. Her eyes sparkle and she sways slightly from side to side as she rushes to express her enthusiasm. It is mesmerizing to watch but I understand her clearly.

Scott also has a passion for France and he is an expert on its wines. Fortunately for us, he has been collecting wine for nearly forty years. When Scott asked me if I wanted to see his cellar, I didn't expect the little room constructed in the basement to be anything that I haven't already seen. After all, I live in a cave and my neighbors have caves that contain thousands of bottles. Even I have about five hundred bottles in my cave. A man's cave says a lot about who he is and quality is the word for Scott's cave. As we walk into a small air-conditioned room in the basement of his villa, I see bottles of Chateau Margaux, Chateau La Tour and some of the great houses of Burgundy. These bottles are labeled with the years 60, 70 and 80. This is a completely new experience for me. In my little corner of France, we are always looking for the wines in bulk that you can buy for seven francs (ninety cents) per liter. A bottle is three quarters of a liter. We are generally pushing the envelope to find a wine for less than seventy-five cents a bottle. Of course my neighbor, Maurice Cheron, will sometimes pull out his foot long brass key to unlock his secret chamber and disappear in the depths of our mountain to pull out a prized bottle but even Maurice cannot match Scott's collection.

Scott asks me what we should have with dinner and I am tempted to say that the 1966 Romanée Conti might go well with pasta but even I would never suggest that I would be worthy drinking these treasures. Luckily, I don't have make the suggestion. Scott pulls out a 1983 Chateau Margaux and a regional wine called Gigondas that he wants me to try. I am quiet happy with his selections. In fact this is enough in itself to justify the twelve-hour drive from our home in Lavardin to Cagnes sur Mer. I never expected more than this but at our next dinner at the villa, Scott brought out two bottles dated 1964 in honor of the year of Aprille's birth. One was a Chateau La Tour which is one of the great houses of Bordeaux. The other bottle was a Chambolle Musigny Les Amoureuses, which is a Burgundy of some renown. Scott said that we would have a taste test but it is impossible for me to compare the two wines or to say one is better than the other. Burgundies are simple elegant wines that remind me of silk and velvet. Bordeaux wines are more complex and require an intelligent palate to fully appreciate. Both these wines are thirty-six years old and Scott says the Chambolle Musigny may be a little over the hill but I can't believe it could be any better than it is.

Provence Notes
Cagnes sur Mer

Cagnes means "an inhabited place on a rounded hill" and is a name of Ligurian[6] origin. If you live in the Alps, you might consider the steep ridges which finger down to the sea in Cagnes to be hills. But it is hard for me to consider these things hills. The ridges form gorges that swallow up errant vehicles that test the narrow switch back roads at high speeds. These roads would be condemned as too dangerous in the States but they are just another amusement ride at the county fair for the French. The land has to be terraced to be used for anything. The villa of our friends, Scott and Nancy McLucas, sits on the top of a ridge with a view of the sea to the south and a view of the Alps to the north. To the southwest, you can see Haut de Cagnes and its fourteenth century chateau.[7] The villa is found at the end of a beautifully landscaped, tree lined path about three hundred meters from the front gate. As one enters the gate, tall, stately cedar trees line the left side of the path while terraced flowerbeds lengthen the right side. The villa is "U" shaped with a courtyard full of flowers and a fountain in the center. There is a swimming pool and balustrade guarding the view to the south. A red tile roof covers the patio where we enjoy the dry, warm air from morning until late at night. This is a perfect venue for sipping a 1964 Chateau La Tour.

---

[6] The Ligurians were shepherds and nomads who lived in the region about 600 B.C.

[7] This chateau was built by Rainier Grimaldi, the Sovereign of Monaco, Admiral of France and Lord of Cagnes. The Grimaldi family remained in possession of the chateau up until the Revolution.

Shortly after arriving at the villa we are introduced to Michel Natale and his son Frederique. Michel is in his early sixties and has worked for Scott for over thirty years. He built most of the villa himself. Fred is about thirty-three years old and has also worked for Scott for many years. Between Michel and Fred, there is nothing that can't be done. The Natale family moved here from Italy many years ago. Many of the natives of this area have an Italian heritage. The Italian border is a short distance away and the people here speak with a strong Italian accent that pleases the ear.

There was one particular event that explains the Italian heritage of this area. Around 1800, a strong wind from the east drove a large number of Italian fishing boats onto the shores of Cros de Cagnes. The fishing was so good here that they decided to stay and brought their families. Of course, Nice and the surrounding area were actually a part of Italy until the late nineteenth century.

Another cultural influence on the coast of Provence is its proximity to North Africa. The influence is not as strong as the Italian but the abundance of Tunisian and Moroccan restaurants shows that it does exist. Scott took us to one of these restaurants in Cros de Cagnes one evening. It is called "La Gazelle D'Or" and couscous is the specialty. I was surprised to learn that this Moroccan restaurant served a Moroccan wine. Morocco is an Islamic country but it produces excellent wine, much like the wine of Provence. We had a rosé and a red that were excellent but the real surprise was the food. Couscous is the specialty of Monsieur Hassan who is the owner and chef. He brought out a large bowl of couscous and a large bowl of soup. These two items are the basics of couscous. Mr. Hassan's couscous is the finest that I have ever tasted. Couscous is just cracked wheat but I have never seen it so fine and tasty. I could have eaten it by itself. The soup is served on the couscous with meat that is traditionally a type of lamb. Monsieur Hassan serves four different types of lamb and each is excellent. Nancy and I were drinking the red wine from Morocco but I tasted the rosé and it might be the better choice with couscous. The name of the rosé is Guerrouane Gris from Les Trois Domaines Appellation d'Origine

Garantie Maroc, imported by Les Celliers de Meknes, 94190 Villeneuve St. Georges. The word gris is often used instead of rosé on labels of wine. Gris is an indication that the wine is a little bit of a cross between a rosé and a white wine. It is not quite dark enough to be a rosé.

Provence Notes
Musée Renoir and Two Stars

Except for the chateau, the Musée Renoir is probably the most important attraction in Cagnes sur Mer. The museum was the home and *atelier* of Auguste Renoir until his death on 3 December 1919. The most striking feature of the museum is the garden with its magnificent olive trees, some of which are hundreds of years old.[8] It is in these gardens that the museum has a sculpture exhibition every two years. Aprille was invited to exhibit a sculpture this year and we are here to complete the installation. She actu-

---

[8] Some people say that these trees are thousands of years old but I was not allowed to count the rings so it can not be confirmed.

ally has two pieces and their installation is somewhat complicated. It is easier to understand by looking at the photographs. They can be seen at her web site (www.aprille.net).

We spent the whole day working on the installation but since she has enlisted the help of Fred Natale, there is little for me to do but admire the art and wander around the grounds. I went to the gift shop to buy some post cards. After selecting about ten cards to send to friends, I approached the counter to pay. A very nice lady told me that the shop was closed and I would have to leave. I looked at my watch and noticed that it was noon. I put the cards back and left because I have seen this phenomena before. It is same all over France. If the shop closes at noon, the clerk closes the cash register exactly at 12:00 P.M. and asks everybody to leave. If it were some disgruntled employee, it would be easier to understand. But I have seen owners' of shops do the same. Even if you are standing there with money in hand, you are asked to leave. Many businesses open at ten o'clock, close at noon for a two-hour lunch and open again at two or sometimes three o'clock. Then again at six o'clock they are hustling the paying customers out the door. These little businesses would not last a week in the States.

There is one industry in France that is an exception to the "close the door in their face" rule. It is the food industry. Any business dealing with food has a completely different set of standards. The owners and employees of food-type businesses work long grueling schedules and they are almost always friendly and solicitous to the customers. Bakers work almost around the clock and stay open to suit the convenience of their customers. Farmers work long days and often can be seen in the fields at sundown. Restaurant employees start early in the morning and work until late at night. Chef Paul van Gessel at Relais d'Antan in Lavardin often talks about how his little restaurant is a step down from the high-pressure work of those seeking stars from the Michelin Guide. There may not be as much pressure, but I see him working from early in the morning to late at night every day except his one day off on Tuesday. It must be truly brutal to maintain a two star restaurant like Restaurant Jacques Maximin in the village of Vence near Cagnes. Everything has to be raised to a higher level of excellence to gain a star. The first thing that I notice as Scott drives us onto the grounds of the restaurant is the number of people providing service. A young man opens the door for us and parks the car. A young lady greets us and shows us to our table without even asking for a name. We are seated on a softly lit terrace where well-dressed waiters and waitresses are swarming like an army of bees who know exactly what has to be done. Everything is impeccable but it seems to be perfection without effort. Everyone and everything is smooth and seamless. The menu is artistically written in long hand. There are three basic menus that range in price from fifty to one hundred dollars. Nancy and I order the menu *Mer et Jardin D'Eté*. Aprille orders the menu *Epices et Saveurs du "Midi"*. And Scott orders the *Grand Menu Homard (Bleu Européen) au Trois Services*. Here are the details of what Nancy and I ordered.

Menu Mer et Jardin D'Eté

Foie gras frais de canard poché au torchon "fait maison" farci aux girolles fraiches gelie Nature, asperges au points, Salades Herbées.

———

Filet de Loup du pays (sauvage) rôti Niçoise, aux pleurots confits et beurre d'anchois.

———

Selle D'agneau(Selle, mignon, rognon) aux cêpes frais et petits oignons aux saisais, jus aux olives noires.

———

Fromages

———

Millefeuille au citron, chocolat, framboises, sauce chocolat lactée, sorbet fruits rouges, petits fours.

Scott ordered a 1998 rosé from Domain Gavoty, Cuvée Clarendon, for the entrée and the fish course. This is a local wine and it is excellent. He ordered a red for the main course and the cheese and though I did not see the label, I believe it was a Gigondas. I hesitate to say that a mistake was made but there was a small deviation that I would describe as wonderful. Nancy and I were served the entrée from Aprille's menu and I believe that Aprille got our entrée (foie gras). What Nancy and I got was *Soupe de tomates crues aux queues D'Ecrevisses, amandes fraiches, Basilic, croûtons, oignons, Vinaigre de Xérès*. It was a cold soup and it was one of those food memories that stays forever. I will try to find it again or maybe try preparating it at home. It looks like chopped tomatoes, shrimp tails, fresh chopped almonds, basil, croutons, chopped onions and Sherry vinegar.

Soupe de tomates crues aux queues D'Ecrevisses

Ingredients:
Peeled chopped tomatoes
Shrimp tails
Sliced almonds
Basil
Chopped onions
Croutons
Sherry vinegar
Directions:
   Mix the ingredients together and serve chilled.

Provence Notes
Bouillabaisse

American recipes for bouillabaisse are nothing like the real thing. True *provençal* bouillabaisse is basically three or four different types of Mediterranean fish, a fish soup and a garlic sauce that you eat on toast. It is not a soup filled with seafood as one often sees in the States. The fish are poached in the soup and served separately. Bouillabaisse originally came from Marseilles where fishermen in the old fishing port developed the dish as a way of using up the less desirable part of their catch. The more tender of these less desirable fish are used to make the soup. The fish with the more tender flesh are served whole or filleted and served separately. Saffron is the soul of bouillabaisse and is used in the soup. Saffron is said to calm coughs and *exciter à l'amour*. If saffron is the soul, *la rouille* is the heart of this dish. This strong tasting garlic sauce is also served separately and is eaten on toast points.

The way that bouillabaisse is served is basically the same with some small variations. Aprille and I had bouillabaisse for the first time about seven years ago in Aix-en-Provence. The fish were served whole and the plates spread out over two tables. It was very difficult to separate the meat from the fish, which are somewhat bony, and the whole consumption process was complicated. Our waiter had to stand nearby and give directions. We tried to make bouillabaisse at home once and discovered that it is very complicated, time consuming and certain ingredients like the fish are impossible to find. Saffron, which is essential, is sold in little pouches like gold dust and is very expensive.

We had bouillabaisse this summer at Relais d'Antan. Chef Paul Van Gessel obtained two Michelin stars for the Petit Nice restaurant in Marseilles in 1979 and knows the subject well. The big difference in Paul's presentation is that he fillets the fish before serving it. There is something lost in the spectacle of the meal but it is well worth it for me. I really enjoyed bouillabaisse for the first time.

When Scott said that he was taking us to Cros de Cagnes for bouillabaisse, I was ready to try it again. When we entered the restaurant, I could tell the atmosphere was different from most French restaurants. French waiters are usually very formal and maybe a little stiff. This restaurant reflects the area's Italian influence. The waiters are animated with waving arms and theatrical gestures. As we are being seated with great fanfare, the owner arrives to greet Scott who is well known here and insists that we have aperitifs and an entrée. Scott says yes for the aperitifs but suggests that since we are having bouillabaisse maybe we will skip the entrées. When you use words like "suggest" and "maybe" in an Italian restaurant, the waiters take this as a coquettish way of saying "feed me everything you have". Our waiters[9] brought out two huge platters of oysters, shrimp, bisques, terrines and things stuffed with crab. We shared these delights along with a bottle of white Cassis that was dry and tasted a little like a Muscadet. When the bouillabaisse was ready the waiters brought out the whole fish to show us what was going to be served. Then the fish were taken back to the kitchen to be filleted by the chef. Next, the filleted fish were served along with the soup, the *rouille* and toast. Of course everything was served with great fanfare and animation. It may be just the general atmosphere of this place but I believe that this is the best presentation of bouillabaisse that I have seen. It was certainly the most fun.

As we are leaving Aprille spotted a newspaper article with a review of the restaurant. It had a picture of the reviewer and the actor Roger Moore. The article said that Roger Moore had recommended this restaurant to

---

[9] I think that we all had our own personal waiter.

the reviewer because of its food and its authentic atmosphere. The article said that some of the high priced restaurants in Nice lacked this authentic quality. As we stand in the foyer, the two brothers who own the restaurant are effusively thanking Scott for his patronage. When Scott mentions something about taxes, one of the brothers starts an obviously practiced spiel: "When I go to city hall to pay my taxes every Thursday, I don't see any Communist, Catholics or Fascists, I don't see any Arabs, Africans or immigrants. It is just people like me." As we walk out the door, I recall a quote from the menu of the two star restaurant of Jacques Maximin:

Je ne m'intéresse
plus qu'à ce qui est vrai,
sincère, pur, large,
en un seul mot,
l'Authentique
      Marcel Pagnol

I also am interested in what is authentic but you never know where you will find it. It is the search and the discovery that is most important. All good things.

Provence Notes
Col de Vence

Fred does not race anymore but he still loves the sport and has the ability. I can tell by the fluid movement of the little French car up the winding goat path of a road. He is going much faster than I would ever dream of trying on this narrow mountain road with no guardrails and lots of distance between the edge and the bottom. Gorge is what it is called here in Provence. I know instinctively that I shouldn't ask the question but like a lemming heading for the sea I must. "Is this what it is like in a rally? No. It is more like this......aaaaaaaaaaaahhhh hhhhhhhhhhhhhhhh". Now I know what a ricocheting bullet feels like when it leaves the gun. In a race, a driver has to keep this pace up for about twelve hours. The stress must be incredible. Especially for a passenger.

Most of the day was more peaceful. Even Fred can't and doesn't care to speed over the roads we traversed today. We are on the Col de Vence. Col is the French word for mountain pass. It is like a desert of rocks here. These great white rocks spread out for miles and cover every inch of the ground except for the paths and depressions cleared by shepherds thousands of years ago. The paths are rare but every depression and hole has been carefully cleared of stones. It is the placement of the stones that makes this place so fascinating. We park the car and hike through these fields where Fred spent his weekends as a young boy on a horse ranch near here. He says that the odd shaped rocks take on the shapes of monsters at night. They are eerie in daylight and the ghosts of their past are everywhere.

Some ancient culture stacked the smaller rocks in shapes and forms that only they would know why. There are walls, cairns, corners, dolmens, menhirs and random piles. No one knows who made these structures or when and why. One can only speculate. This is sheep herding country so the piles could have been shelters at one time. The speculation is that the forms were made over two thousand years ago but no one knows for certain. The sheepherders still use this land for grazing but there is little else here. The place is obviously dear to Fred because of fond childhood memories, but I think he finds a deeper connection to his past and his ancestors among these rocks. Fred is a native, which is rare to find in any part of France but especially in Provence. As he stares at the mountain to the south, he says that he has still not climbed that one. It is more of a statement of what he has accomplished because he has climbed the others. I suspect that he does not want to use up the final mystery of this holy place. It would be like knowing the truth about your religion. Then it would no longer be a religion.

We climb back into the car and head further into the depths of this mountain pass. The remarkable thing about this area is that there are so few buildings here. There is an occasional shepherd's stone shelter but very little else. We come to a crossroads and take a left on a road made of small boulders. Fred bounces the car from boulder to boulder like a child hopping on stones to cross a creek. After about a kilometer of road that would break most four-wheel drive vehicles we find a place in the road that the

Audi cannot traverse. Fred says it is too bad because he wanted to show us the Gorge du Loup with a view of the village of Gourdon. Aprille spots an elk high up on the ridge and we get out of the car to watch it. We decide to walk to the Gorge, which is about one more kilometer. The walk is worth the hike. The Gorge du Loup is a straight drop off from the trail. The view is incredible and Fred points out Gourdon in the distance which is barely visible in the haze. Fred says that it is clearer in winter. I find a Grande Randonnée marker that Fred says is GR4 or GR51. He says that this trail, which winds down the mountain, was one of the main routes from the high Alps to the sea for hundreds and maybe thousands of years.

As we are returning to the car, Fred spots three large elk high on the ridge. They stare at us as we hike this ancient trail back to the car. I don't want to leave. I like it here and envy Fred and his childhood in this special place.

Fall

Sunflowers extend their lives into early September but when they begin to lose their color and turn black, fall has arrived. Fall is a time when flowers begin to disappear and everything is faded and brown. But it is not a time of sadness. Indeed, it is the season of the harvest and there is a feeling of abundance everywhere.

Fall is the critical time for the winegrower. There is no other time of the year when the weather is so important. If September is cold and wet, the wine will not be good. If there is sunshine and warm weather, *à la tienne* will echo from the caves in the spring. But it is not necessary to wait until spring to taste the wine. Within two weeks of putting the wine in the barrels, it turns into a milky white or pink liquid called *Bernache*. This is the local name for *vin nouveau* and it is enjoyed by all for just two weeks before it clears and begins to develop its own unique character as wine.

Bernache still has the sweet taste of grape juice but it is fully loaded with the same alcohol content of wine.

Just a few years ago every little farm in the valley had a few rows of vines and all the caves would come to life by October. The grape harvest was hard but always a time of fellowship and communion with a neighbor. Although this tradition still exists, many of the small farms are pulling up their vines as the farmers grow older.

By October all the cave chimneys are puffing smoke as men and women roast chestnuts over the fire and sip *Bernache*. Lit fireplaces multiply as the days get shorter and the smell of roasting meat permeates the air.

By November the shorter days are more noticeable and the weather begins to turn cooler. The fireplace is still the symbol of hearth and home, and an important source of heat for most homes. Every evening is like Thanksgiving with the sizzling sound of fat dripping into the fire from large turkeys, pheasants or legs of lamb spinning on a string.

Fall is also the start of hunting season and the far off sound of hunting horns and barking dogs provide background for the savage ballet of running animals in the woods and plains above the river. Wild game is always on the menu. *Cheveuil* (deer), *sanglier* (wild boar), pheasant, quail and duck are served in a sauce with potatoes, onions and wild mushrooms. Fall is truly a time of abundance.

L'Alambic
(The Still)

There is nothing quite so impressive as *l'alambic* with all its shining copper, spinning tubes and hissing steam. It is a circus for children and a shrine to Dionysus for the men who bring their *marc*, cherries, plums, apples and pears for conversion into *goutte (eau-de-vie)*. Actually, women and children rarely see the circus anymore. Fifty years ago the *distillateur ambulant* or *bouilleur ambulant* still pulled his copper monster with horses and parked it under the most convenient shade tree to sell his services. It must have been a show for all to see in every village he visited. Much has changed but much has remained the same. The *alambic* is still the same impressive fire breathing copper monster but the outdoor shows under the shade trees are a thing of the past. It has all moved indoors into a metal building with a concrete floor and an evacuation pool in back. But the ambulatory nature of the trade remains the same. Our local *distillateur ambulant* is Jacky Rochereau and he is getting ready to move to one of the other three locations where he is always in demand.

When Monsieur Jean told me that Jacky was leaving his building on the border between St. Rimay and Villavard for the care and maintenance of some foreign neighbors near Tours, I ask if I could get some pictures of the still before he left. Jacky is a cousin of Monsieur Jean, a fact that Jean seems to be proud of. Why not? Jacky turns ordinary fermented fruit into something more vital than gasoline in the Loir and Cher, *eau-de-vie*.

The consumption of *eau-de-vie* has been a concern of the French government for many years. I read somewhere that the French drink more alcohol that any other country. I can believe this when I see the energy and ingenuity that goes into making *pousse d'épine, feuille de pêcher, écorce de clementine, vin côt, marc, eau-de-vie* and a dozen other concoctions that I have tried. On the other hand, the French don't seem to get drunk like Americans. The bars in France are civilized places where men come in for a *coup* then leave after appropriate salutations. In America, bars are where you go to get drunk, fight, die or meet someone that you never want to see again. Despite the French reputation for moderation, alcoholism is rising and the government is attempting to address the problem. Last summer I learned that you can't buy wine at the restaurants on the autoroute unless you buy something to eat. *C'est dur.*

The regulation of the distillery business has been going on for more than two hundred years and it is still strictly regulated today. Each family is entitled to only ten liters of pure alcohol or twenty liters of fifty percent alcohol. The product that drips out of the spout on Jacky's *alambic* is usually about fifty percent alcohol and Jacky keeps detailed paperwork on his clients. The law requires it. At one time the government tried to phase out this whole distillery business but it didn't work. It is one of those traditions in France that the people will not let go of and since the Revolution the government has a tendency to listen to the people.

Jacky's *alambic* business is obviously a male environment. Although women will occasionally invade this domain, men have been known to become board certified in gynecology just from looking at the calendars on the walls. It is no longer a circus for children but the *alambic* is still entertainment for adults. Everyone who walks in sticks a finger under the dripping spout for a taste. Usually it just tastes like firewater to me, but today the drops have a distinct taste of gamay. Jacky tells me that it is *eau-de-vie de marc*. *Marc* is what is left after the grapes are pressed. It is the skin, seeds and stems that are left in the wine press. Nothing is wasted here. Memories of war and starvation still influence the people of Europe.

When the distillation process is complete, Jacky vents the steam from the vat chamber and spins the huge copper wing nuts to open the top. He pours the dregs of grape skins, stems and seeds with remaining liquid in a square concrete vat which flows into a retaining pond in the rear of the building. It is like witnessing infinity. These grapes have finally finished their usefulness. I would like to ask what he does with the stuff in the retaining pond but I don't want to hear the answer. I prefer to think of Jacky's still as infinity and beyond.

La Vendange

Mon pauvre verre, tu es vide. Je te plein.
Mon pauvre verre, tu es plein. Je te vide.
                              Maryvonne Cassard

Vendange is the French word for wine grape harvest. The fact that there is a special word for the harvesting of wine grapes is an indication of the importance of wine in this country. Before the introduction of the harvesting machines in 1983, all the harvesting was done by hand. Even though it was back breaking work, it was such a popular event in Europe that people would come from all over the world to participate. The only remuneration was wine, dinner and fellowship. Once the harvest was complete, there would be a truly big party with a last meal and then a harvest ball in the local village. Some vineyards still harvest by hand for reasons of *appellation* or for reasons of quality.[10] There is a real need for

---

[10] Some wine connoisseurs don't like the taste of escargot and worms in their cabernet.

workers in these vineyards and the French government requires payment of social security and minimum wages. If the wine grower has to pay for your labor, he is probably going to want you to pick a few grapes. This takes some of the fun out of the outing because it becomes a job and back-breaking work.

Nevertheless, Aprille and I made arrangements to go to Vouvray to help with *la vendange*. Our friend Jean Montambaux warned us that it would be a long, hard day and the weather in October can be freezing and wet. The commercial vineyards can't afford to stop work because of the weather. In fact, bad weather necessitates that the work go more quickly. If we go, we will be committed to a long, hard day of work. Jean was so worried about our going that he made arrangements for us to try a *vendange* at a private vineyard in Saint Rimay.

We are seven for *la vendange*. The magnificent seven includes Jean Montambaux *ledit* Monsieur Jean, André Desneux *ledit* P'tit Jules, Roger Gillard *ledit Patron*, Thierry *ledit Vraie Force* and Janine *ladite Derviche Tourneur*, Aprille *ladite Kid* and me *ledit Mal à Dos*. Actually, we are nine but the magnificent nine doesn't really work. I don't count Orphelie who is only four years old and her grandfather who brought her to observe this sacred ritual.

The P'tit Jules and the Patron own a small vineyard above the infamous tunnel of Saint Rimay where Hitler parked his train in October 1940, while meeting with Maréchal Petain in Montoire-sur-Loir. These are the vines that we are going to harvest. We all gather at André's small farm in the center of St. Rimay at eight-thirty in the morning to discuss the weather, which is somber at the moment. Since it is not raining, a decision is made to start the harvest. Aprille asks if she can ride on the trailer behind the tractor. I ride with Monsieur Jean who never stops cracking jokes and laughing. As I see Aprille bouncing and laughing high on the trailer, I get the sense that this is not truly serious. This sense heightens as André begins to swerve his Columbo like car from side to side on the road.

Jean follows the serpentine line as we watch Dirk, André's German shepherd, smile with pleasure to have his head in the wind.

When we reach the vineyard, André hands each of us a bucket and a pair of clippers. The humor ends here as I bend over and cut a bunch of grapes. Back breaking work is really an understatement for this type of labor, but as I warm up the work gets easier. We are picking pineau d'aunis today and we will be making a rosé wine. After we fill our buckets, we empty them into the *hotte*[11] carried by Thierry. He hauls the *hotte* to the trailer and dumps it in the bin. We harvest two and one half rows of grapes, which takes about one hour. The other two and one half rows belong to someone else or will be used for making another type of wine. We are finished with this field, so naturally we have to drink a bottle of pineau d'aunis to celebrate the accomplishment. We all share the bottle from two glasses that are passed around like peace pipes.

After a brief discussion on the quality of this bottle, we head to another vineyard. Here the picking is more difficult because there are two different types of grapes planted in the rows and it is difficult to tell one from another. Orphelie arrives with her grandfather and wants to fill her little bucket. She says over and over "*Je fais la bernache*". We manage to finish two rows by 11:30 a.m. and celebrate again with another bottle. We load up our buckets and clippers and head back to the farm. Getting back to the farm is also an event to be celebrated so we all stand around a large barrel where André pours a bottle of Vouvray to quench our thirst. Everyone is anxious to take off for lunch but André insists that we try his *pousse d'épine* before leaving. I think that we are drinking more wine than we will produce with our harvest, but that does not seem to be important. We are told that we can come back in the afternoon if we want to watch the pressing of the grapes.

---

[11] A basket worn like a backpack that is used to carry the grapes from the pickers to the wagon.

I am a little surprised at the simplicity of making white wine. The commercial vineyards probably do it differently but these small farmers still do things the traditional way. We put the grapes in the *pressoir* and squeeze the juice into a vat. The liquid comes out a light pink color, but this is the same method for making white wine. The juice goes directly from the vat to large 220 liter barrels where it will turn to *bernache* in about six days.

Bernache is the sweet, fizzy *vin nouveau* that lasts only about a week to ten days and is drunk with chestnuts roasted over fireplaces in the caves along the Loir River. A week or two later it will loose its sweet, fizzy character and will begin to turn into wine. The fermentation process will last about six weeks but the wine is not mature for bottling until April or May. During the six-month period of maturation in the barrels the wine is transferred to other barrels in order to separate the dregs that have settled to the bottom. This *tirage*[12] is done three times and the timing depends on the circumstances. It is a very simple process.

We are making *biscandine* which is a white wine that is lightly pink. The color is the result of the red pineau d'aunis grape that we harvested. The same grape can be used to make a red wine but the process is a little different. The traditional method involved crushing the grapes with a wooden pole before pouring them in a *cuve* or vat. Once in the vat they were crushed again with the feet three times during the first day and two times during the following days. After a week in the cuve, the juice is poured in barrels. The *marc* (stems, seeds and hulls) is put in the pressoir and squeezed for the last of the juice. The *marc* is saved for making a type of eau-de-vie or brandy.

---

[12] *Tirage* is the act of drawing the wine off the upper part of the barrel to separate it from the dregs which have settled to the bottom.

The Dog Behind The Iron Mask

France has the largest number of dog owners per capita in the world. Americans love dogs too but the two cultures are completely different in their respective affections. Americans like large, mean dogs that eat babies and have to be executed. There are no pitbulls in France. French dogs tend to be small and elegant. They are the kings and queens of the household and generally not much bigger than a cat. These princely animals live a life of leisure but there are also a few less-privileged outdoor dogs that *monte la garde*. Guard dogs bark continuously everywhere in France but the wagging tails belie their true nature. I have hiked all over France and never had a problem with dogs. In the States, every neighborhood has a problem dog. Dogs tend to be like their masters and in this older, more mature culture, the dogs are less aggressive.

Dogs tend to take on the personalities and appearances of their masters. It is hard to say that Pete and Manny look alike because Manny is a small, pedigreed dachshund and Pete is a large man with a passion for life and adventure. If Pete reads an article about hiking in the Nepal, he doesn't dream about it. He goes and does it. He worked for IBM for thirty years and is now retired, but he has not slowed down. He has traveled all over the world and is always working on unexplored places. Manny, on the other hand, is definitely a French lapdog and king of Pete's household. The similarity between Pete and Manny is in the eyes. They both have a searching look as if they are living in the immediate future just over the next hill or around the next curve. When I reached down to greet Manny for the first time, he took on that strange distant look and refused to respond. My friend Scott said, "No, no. Manny is a not a comer." He is a little too regal to be a comer. He is a true prince.

When Pete told us the real history of Manny, it reminded me of the the man behind the iron mask. "The man behind the iron mask" was a sub-plot in one of the novels of Alexandre Dumas that followed *The Three Mousqueteers*. Hollywood tried to make a movie of the stories several times but just never managed to get the story right. The real story involved a twin brother of Louis XIV who at birth was spirited away by the evil Cardinal Marazin for political reasons. A group who opposed Louis dis-covered the twin and plotted to place him on the throne. The plot was foiled and Louis had his twin bother secretly imprisoned and an unremov-able iron mask placed over his face. The crime of *lèse-majest*é (a crime against a sovereign) is punishable by death but Louis did not want any publicity of the existence of his twin.

The story of Manny is quite similar . I met Manny and Pete for the first time when they climbed into my car outside the small *provençal* village of La Gaude. We were heading out from Cagnes on the coast with our mutual friend, Scott, to hike up a small mountain called the *Baou de la Gaude*. Baou is what the natives call these pre-alp hills, but after looking up at the rocky peak from the village below, this *baou* looked like a moun-tain. Manny has been moaning in anticipation of this hike all morning and stretches the limits of his leash when we start up the hill. The air is heavy with the smell of brume, a yellow flowering bush that is in abun-dance here. There is also the light scent of thyme, rosemary and sage in the late summer breeze. Most of the walk is on the open sunny hillside where you can see the hazy blue Mediterranean sea to the south and the snowy triangles of the Italian Alps to the east. To the north the violet-gray cliffs of the pre-alps jut out like great prows of stony ships in the deep blue of a *provençal* sky as we switched-back up the trail. Manny keeps us amused as he struts up the path like a dog four times his size. The trail is called *La promenade du Grand Chêne* (The Trail of the Great Oak) because it termi-nates in a kind of depression where an enormous oak tree is surrounded by stones that some ancient culture has stacked in a circle. The stones are stacked everywhere in circles, piles, lines and walls. These crude structures are so old that no one knows their origin. After the bright sun of the trail it is leafy, cool and a perfect place to hear a good story.

While sitting under the oak tree taking a water break, Pete tells us the story of Manny, a/k/a Merlin. Pete and his wife, Claude, ordered a thoroughbred dachshund from a breeder in Brittany. After paying the $800 dollar charge, a tiny pedigree puppy arrived in the mail with his papers. Thoroughbred kennels name their dogs when they are born and issue official certificates that give the name and other important details of their breeding pedigree. The dog's name was Emmanuel. Pete took a quick peek at his new dog and went to work. Pete, who was working for IBM in the south of France at the time, received a frantic afternoon call to come back home immediately. Claude told him that something had happened to Emmanuel but wouldn't say anything else. When Pete arrived, he found the dog dead. Evidently, his mother-in-law had accidentally stepped on Manny and killed the puppy instantly. This was a traumatic event for the ladies and neither was able to accept the cold reality of the puppy's death. The previous dog had a family burial complete with flowers and a marked grave, but it had started to rain and everyone was in denial. Pete decided to handle the burial quietly by himself without ceremony.

He phoned the kennel that same night and ordered another dog. There was one last puppy in the litter and he arrived the next day by special delivery. Because the new dog arrived in a rush the kennel forgot to send his papers, Pete committed *lèse-majesté* by calling the new dog Emmanuel, or Manny for short, and placed him on the real Emmanuel's throne. The throne was a personalized Land's End dog bed with Emmanuel stitched on one side. The whole family fell in love with Manny and the trauma of his elder brother's sad demise was forgotten.

No one thought much about Manny's official papers until Claude and Pete met a couple who breed dachshunds. Pete is justifiably proud of Manny and he started seriously considering breeding his fine prince. He called the kennel in Brittany and asked for Manny's papers. When the papers arrived, he discovered that Manny's real name is Merlin. Enough years and happy dog memories have passed for Manny's transfiguration to be forgotten. Manny's official papers say that his name is Merlin but only Pete knows where the papers are hidden. Except for the occasional eerie organ music coming from the attic, there is no evidence of a twin dachshund in La Gaude, but there have been rumors of a dachshund wearing an iron mask in a dog pound near Nice.

The Best I Ever Had

Aprille and I were invited to a kind of potluck dinner last summer. It was one of those perfect summer nights when daylight lasts until eleven o'clock. All the guests sat at one long table along the bank of the river. Dinner was *à la bonne franquette* (something simple) but most of the women brought their own special desserts as if it were a competition.

Maybe it was just my imagination but during a conversation with the lady across from me, I got the distinct impression that she wanted to have sex with me. Then Aprille tapped me on the shoulder and asked me:

"What did you say to that lady?"

"Why do you ask dear?" I replied.

"Well, she looks like she wants to have sex with you."

Well, I guess it was not just my imagination after all. I had just told the lady that her *Tarte Tatin* was the best I ever had. Americans love apple pie but this little scene demonstrates how important it is to the French. It is one of those things so seminally basic to a culture that it evokes emotions just a touch carnal.

Apple pie has long been a symbol of American-ness but *Tarte Tatin* is strictly French. It is basically apple pie baked upside down and served hot. It was invented by a clumsy cook in the village of Lemotte Beuvron in the Sologne region of France. Stephanie Tatin already had a reputation for being an outstanding cook before she and her sister, Caroline, took over the ownership of the Hotel Tatin in 1888. Stephanie, who had a reputation for not being very bright, managed the kitchen while Caroline dealt with the guests and managed the hotel.

Apple pie was Stephanie's specialty and she always served it perfectly crusty, caramelized and ready to melt in the mouth. But life was not easy for her, because she worked from early in the morning until late at night over her hot ovens and copper pans. One particularly busy day during hunting season, she was startled by gunshots and turned the pie upside down. She went ahead and put it in the oven wrong side up and then served this strange dessert without giving it time to cool. It was delicious and became popular all over France under the name of *Tarte Tatin.*

Tarte Tatin is taken so seriously in France that a brotherhood was founded to protect the true secret of preparing this dish and to promote its consumption. It is called *La Confrerie des Lichonneux de Tarte Tatin.* The *Grande Maître du Secret* published the above recipe so it is not really a secret. The true purpose of the association is to protect the original recipe from being perverted by people who want to put ice cream on top.

There is an annual celebration to honor and defend the origin of Tarte Tatin and to induct new members to the Brotherhood. The last celebration was in September. I hope to attend the next celebration to sample the traditional *Tarte Tatin* and compliment the *cuisinières.* Check the official website of *Tarte Tatin* for the next event and how to join. http://www.tarte-tatin.com/.

Tarte Tatin

Ingredients:
150 grams of butter
125 grams of sugar
1   Kilo of apples
1   Pie pastry
Directions:
   Butter a high-sided pie pan with 150 grams of butter.
Sprinkle 125 grams if sugar on the butter.
Peel 1 Kilo of apples. Cut them in quarters and place them side by side with the curved side down. Fill the gaps with larger slices of apple.

Start cooking on a low flame for 10 to 15 minutes to monitor the beginning of the caramelizing. After caramelized to your taste, place it in the oven at 200 C (400 F)for 1/4 of an hour.

Take the pie out of the oven and arrange the pie pastry slightly larger that the pie pan over the top. Put it back in the oven for approximately 1/4 of an hour.

Once cooking is finished, take it out of the oven and allow it to sit for a few minutes. Place a serving dish over the pie pan and turn it over quickly. Serve it as is.

The apples will be impregnated with the natural caramel resulting from the combination of the cooked sugar, butter and the juice of the apples, taking on the smoothness and exceptional taste that characterizes the genuine Tarte Tatin.

Le P'tit Jules

He is not the mayor of Saint Rimay but he is the true lord of the manor in this little town. *Le P'tit Jules*, also known as, André Desneux lives in his grandfather's house across the street from the old barn that he was born in seventy-five years ago. He barely stretches above five feet and is round as a beach ball, but he possesses that mysterious phenomenon sometimes called presence. He literally reigns over his domain with calm and grace. He daily dons his blue worker's uniform and *casquette* like a bishop's chasuble and mitre. His presence is so palpable that we have renamed his cave the Prieuré d'Epine and Monsieur Jean now calls him the Curé. A *prieuré* is a church and *épine* refers to a plant used to flavor *pousse d'épine*, an aperitif made locally. Of course Monsieur Jean prays daily at André's cave and we also make frequent stops.

It is not possible to pass his cave without stopping to pay homage. In fact, I discovered that it is a sin not to stop. I was passing by his cave everyday on my way to and from the library in Vendôme. After a week of committing this sin, Monsieur Jean came by to tell me that André was very upset that I was not stopping on my way to and from the library. I explained that going to the library was like going to a job for me and that I couldn't stop and get drunk on my way to work everyday. Jean just hunched his shoulders as if to say, "I don't make the rules, I just warn of their infringement." I now snake my way to Vendôme by some back roads traversed only by a few sheep and cows. On the way back, I stop and pray.

André's cave is unusual because it is dug into the ground and reinforced with concrete blocks so it is squared off and lacks the round, uneven look of other caves in this area. But everything else is traditional and at the same time unique. At first I could not understand why all these the old caves are covered with soot and charcoal. The ceiling and walls of Andre's cave looks like a fire burned hot here once. Many caves in this area have this sooty look. After burning candles in our cave, I began to understand. These caves are hundreds of years old so candles, kerosene lamps and torches lit these dark holes for many years before electricity. Also, the huge oak barrels that stretch the hundred-foot length of this cave had to be sterilized once a year with burning sulfur which added to the char. There is a look of organized chaos here. There are barrels, bottles, baskets, corks, *hottes,* pipes, pipettes and odd-looking tools everywhere. Everything is old and coated with dust and mold. Even the sole bare light bulb above the makeshift bar looks like it was made in the1920's.

The darkness, the dust and the smell of fermentation could be depressing but it is not. There is a sense of conviviality that helps, but the real contrast to all this moldy darkness strikes like a hallelujah chorus though a sunny window when André uncorks a bottle of Vouvray. There is a second chorus for a glass of *pousse d'épine* and the sky literally opens when he breaks out his newest concoction. In a large clay vessel called a *saloir*, he removes the lid and shows us a dark rosé liquid that he calls *écorce de clementine*. It is much like *pousse d'épine* but made with the skin of tangerines. The flavor is sweet, spicy and bitter at the same time. Aprille likes this aperitif so much that she designed and made André some labels to put on his bottles. Here is the formula.

In a large container add the following:

Ecorce de Clementine

Ingredients:
5 liters of a good rosé wine of 12% alcohol
1 liter of goûtte (eau-de-vie) at 40% alcohol
2 lbs. of sugar
The zest and juice of 10 tangerines
Directions:
Put all of the ingredients in a 10 liter container. Stir the contents once a day for about two weeks. Leave covered for 40 days. Strain, bottle and serve cold.
Let there be light.

Mersault

Cardinal de Berry, a seventeenth century *protégé* of Madame de Montespan, served only fine Meursault at mass, *pour ne pas faire la grimace devant Le Seigneur.* He was quite concerned about the royal family accidentally grimacing at their Lord and Savior from a poor communion wine.

The village of Meursault sits in Burgundy beside its more famous neighbor, Montrachet. It produces mostly white wines. Although it has no Grand Cru, its reputation for excellence goes back hundreds of years. Meursault wines are notable for the taste of hazelnut. It has been described as a sensual wine of finesse and frankness.

My first trip to Meursault was on one of those dark, wet and somber European afternoons when an over-imaginative mind worries that our friendly-foursome might make faces before God soon unless we find a

Meursault double quick. Aprille, the designated driver, has been white-knuckle touring in a cloudburst long enough. Since we know nothing about the village, we stop at the first *dégustation* sign that we see.

As we enter the gate, a young man in orange rain gear directs us to the tasting cave. We enter a narrow room claustrophobically full of wine cases. At the bar in the back I see an American couple trying the Cardinal's grimace killers. I know that they are Americans immediately. They are tall, well-dressed and bright-eyed. They possess that particularly American nervous energy. The man serving is definitely French. He is relaxed and ready to pour for the world as it is presented to him. Brian and Catherine Potts from Boston have tasted a glass of petit Meursault from the cellar of Monsieur Guy Bocard and are ready to leave. They have a schedule to keep and have no idea that Monsieur Bocard expects them to try about nine different wines and he is saving his best for the last. He could care less if they actually buy a bottle. It is show time and all he wants is an audience. Brian asks me to explain to him that they can buy his wine in Boston and that they have to leave.

I explain the situation to Monsieur Bocard who isn't really listening because he is warming up to his enlarged audience. Mitchell, Nadine and Aprille are oohing and aahing over their first glass. Brain agrees to try one more glass of the oohing vintage but Catherine says no because she is driving. She tries to hand back her glass and finds it refilled instead. This is the first of the Premier Crus and the start of a liquid Babette's feast. By the time we get to the third glass no one is protesting and everyone is talking about fruit, vanilla and character.

Monsieur Bocard asks if we would like to see his cellar and we all descend into a cave full of oak barrels stacked four high. The room is quite warm for a cave on a cold wet day. He explains it's the heat from the fermenting wine. There is a light sweet smell of fermenting grapes. He is obviously pleased with our interest and answers all my questions with enthusiasm. He invites us to return to the tasting room where we try one last bottle.

His *pièce de résistance* is a bottle of Les Charmes Premier Cru, and as the wine is poured somehow Catherine's glass doesn't get filled. Brian automatically starts to tell Monsieur Bocard she doesn't want any more but a laughing Catherine already has her glass under the bottle. They wind up buying three bottles after seriously considering a case. Our friends buy three more. The six of us run through the rain to our cars and our schedules. It is still dark, cold and somber but everyone is grinning from ear to ear. Cardinal de Berry would be proud today.

Reliquary

Practically every village in France has or had some holy object in a reliquary in its church. Reliquaries are display cases that house holy relics for the faithful. The relics themselves range from the macabre to merely odd. There are bones, eyeballs, fingernails, hairs, veils and shrouds everywhere in France. When we visited Illiers-Combray on Valentine's Day, we found a small piece of the veil of the Virgin Mary in the church. When we went to Vézelay last October we touched the reliquary holding the knucklebone of Mary Magdalene. Mary Magdalene is much revered in France and parts of her body can be found in churches everywhere. Her chin bone was at one time in the church of the Madeleine in Vendôme. Madeleine is the French name for Magdalene. Regardless of your religious denomination, getting up close and personal with Mary Magdalene's knucklebone makes an impression.

When I moved to France I knew very little about relics and reliquaries. I don't think they exist in the Protestant religions. Even my American Catholic friends don't seem to know a lot about these things. But the stories behind these relics are fantastic tales of magic, mysticism and superstition. Of course if you were a peasant cured of blindness or the plague from touching the breastbone of Saint Rimay, the stories weren't fairy tales but proof of the power and goodness of God.

In the middle ages a relic could bring economic and religious benefits to an otherwise poor region. A famous relic could attract thousands of pilgrims to a remote village. About 900 years ago, the neighboring village of Montoire-sur-Loir was a booming metropolis because of a wooden statue of Saint Greluchon in the little church of Saint Oustrille. Women would come from near and far to scratch off pieces of the wooden base of the statue with their fingernails. It was believed that a tea made from the wood shavings would make the women fertile. Children born after this pilgrimage were said to have fine, curly hair like the wood shavings that made their birth possible. A local apothecary sold a miracle potion called "greluchine" that was guaranteed to prevent sterility. Commerce thrived in the village from the feeding and housing of the pilgrims. When the court of Louis XIV learned of the celebrated Saint, the pilgrimage came to an end. The nude statute scandalized Louis' mistress so he had the poor Saint dressed up in the robes of a bishop. It destroyed the mystique of the statute and the pilgrims stopped coming. Thus ended one of the most popular pilgrimages in the Vendômois.

Louis XIV seems to have been particularly hard on relics. While on a pilgrimage to Cotignac in the Var, he heard about the celebrated miracle of Sainte Roseline. Sainte Roseline was a thirteenth century sainte whose body was exhumed five years after her burial. The body was found to be still intact by some miracle or natural mummification. Her still living eyeballs were placed in a reliquary in a church in the Var. Louis wanted to know if the eyeballs were really alive so he sent his doctor to examine these relics. The doctor punctured the left eyeball and destroyed it. He reported to Louis that the right eyeball appeared to still be living. This must have been a blow to the faithful of Sainte Roseline who already believed in the miracle and didn't need to destroy the relic to prove its authenticity.

Pilgrims believed that touching a reliquary would put them in communication with the saint who would intercede and communicate their prayers to heaven. There was also a belief that touching the reliquary would heal certain maladies. In Vendôme, the Abbey of the Trinity contained a relic particularly venerated by pilgrims. It was a tear of Jesus Christ contained in a crystal vial. Some very gullible Crusaders bought that tear for a pretty penny from a fast-talking merchant in Jerusalem. Only the Holy Hand Grenade of Antioch was more prized. Actually the tear was a gift from the Emperor of Constantinople to Geoffroy Martel, founder of the Abbey, for his help in chasing the Saracens from the Holy

Land. The vial holding the tear of Jesus Christ was destroyed during the Revolution but it remained in the Abbey from 1042 until it was lost. It made Vendôme a very desirable destination for over 600 years.

Devotion to relics gradually declined, in large part because of well-known cases of fakes. But belief in relics has not disappeared all together. The Shroud of Turin is still revered by thousands despite the controversy surrounding its authenticity. Relics are fascinating and they give life to biblical tales of Christ's Passion and the martyrdom of the saints. After seeing a relic of Saint Rimay, Saint John or whoever, one can't help but…. *wonder.* I suppose that was the point of having relics in the first place.

Sloe Gin

Sloes are small plums sometimes called blackthorns. The French call them *prunelles*. The leaves from this tree are used to make *pousse d'épine* but the fruit has its own uses. The sloes are sometimes used to make *eau-de-vie* or an aperitif called sloe gin.

Ingredients for 2.5 liters:

2.5 liters of gin	*4 pints*
750 grams of ripe, dry sloes	*1 1/2 pounds*
30 grams of almonds, blanched	*1 ounce*
750 grams of sugar	*1 1/2 pounds*

Directions:

Prick the sloes several times with a fork so that the juices and color will be drawn out. Put the sloes in a 4.5 liter (8 pint) jar with the almonds and add the sugar; then pour in the gin, and cover. Shake the jar every three days for three months. Strain off the liquor, bottle it and seal the corks. The gin is ready for use or may be kept for years, improving greatly in the keeping.

Battle of Poitiers

Just the thought of sitting around with Monsieur Jean, Maurice and Marcel drinking tea and eating camel riders sends a chill up my spine. But this could have very easily been the case if Charles Martel had not stopped the Islamic army of Abd al-Rahman in 732 at the Battle of Poitiers just a few miles south of here. I always intended to visit the battlefield one day. After watching Islamic terrorists destroy the World Trade center in New York, I decided to go ahead and make the one-hour drive to this famous battlefield. It all started about 1300 years ago and does not appear to be ending soon.

There are three great battles that carry the name of the Battle of Poitiers and none of them actually occurred at Poitiers. The one that I am interested in was fought 25 October 732 on a plain twenty kilometers north of Poitiers called *Moussais-la-Bataille*. In this battle, Charles Martel defeated the Islamic forces led by Abd al-Rahman and effectively stopped the Muslim expansion into Europe. Several years earlier, Islamic armies from Spain had seized and pillaged the Rhone Valley and Burgundy. The Frankish kingdom was weak and divided at this time but it seemed to find a common goal in stopping the Islamic army and recapturing Bordeaux that the Saracens had seized along with the Aquitaine. Perhaps it was the thought of loosing the *grands crus* of Bordeaux that finally united the French.

The monument at *Moussais-la Bataille* tells the story of the battle, the history of the two religions and the motivations of the opposing forces. It is the history of the two religions that is most interesting to me. At the time of this battle, Christianity was over seven hundred years old and the predominant religion of Europe. Islam was barely a hundred years old but had already spread from the Middle East, across North Africa and into Europe. Christianity, on the other hand, spread slowly and left a trail of martyrs who were canonized after being tortured, decapitated or fed to the lions. There were so many Christian martyrs that it is hard to say that Christianity didn't have true believers but the people of Gaul seem to have converted gradually. So many churches are built on top of dolmens, menhirs and old Roman temples, one gets the impression that Christianity bred with the ancient beliefs rather replacing them. Indeed, the traditions and doctrines of the church have so many pagan foundations that the flexibility of early Christianity seems to have been the key to its success.

The explosive growth of Islam is a different story. In the year 610, a forty-year-old man from Mecca named Mohammed made several visits to nearby Mont Hira where the angel Gabriel appeared and made certain revelations to him. These revelations were later recorded and became the Koran, the word of Allah. Mohammed tried to convert the Meccans to his new monotheistic religion but it didn't go over well with the rich merchants who viewed him as a troublemaker.

Mohammed and his small clan sought refuge in the oasis of Medina 350 kilometers to the northwest. He was able to organize the two Yeminite and three Jewish tribes of Medina into a community. In an attempt to convert the Jews, he adopted their law of fasting on Yom Kippour and praying in the direction of Jerusalem. But the Jews never accepted the Koran and he later exterminated those remaining in Medina. Afterwards, he changed the day of fasting to Ramadan and the direction of prayer changed from Jerusalem to the Ka'ba in Mecca. The Ka'ba is a cube shaped building built by Abraham and Ishmael that contains a black stone supposedly delivered by the angel Gabriel.

After years of war with Mecca, he gained control of the city in the year 630 and destroyed all the pagan idols in the Ka'ba. He declared Abraham the only one true prophet and erased the frescos of all the other prophets. Mohammed believed that Allah favored his war against the unbelievers and he continued his struggle in Syria. He died suddenly in 632 without designating a successor. His achievements seem rather ordinary compared to other religious figures, but within one century Mohammed's followers were close to dominating the world.

There is no record of how many men died at the Battle of Poitiers, but ten years earlier the Duke of Aquitaine defeated a Muslim army near Toulouse where over 350,000 Saracens died. The Battle of Poitiers was an even greater defeat for Islam and eventually led to their retreat behind the Pyrenees. They were eventually pushed out of Spain (1492), but they are still the dominant religion of Africa, the Middle East and Asia. The last census shows that there are over one billion Muslims and two billion Christians. Both religions worship the same God and have their roots in the Old Testament and Judaism, but there are only fifteen million Jews in the world today.

JEAN BAILLEUL
1876 – 1949

The Ghost of Chateau Chèvre

I don't normally believe ghost stories but the story of Chateau Chèvre leaves me cold. The large structure next to our little cave has always fascinated me. All the caves on the Rotte aux Biques are interesting and unique, but Chateau Chèvre is next door so I always wonder what tunnels and deep chambers are abutting the walls of our home. We do hear distant noises from time to time, but we usually know who and where they are coming from.

We have known our neighbors for two years but our social intercourse has been brief, albeit friendly. Monsieur Baroth is an artist from Paris. We usually see him on the weekends or hear him talking to the cats that populate the goat path leading to our cave. He says that he is like a mockingbird because he lives in other people's nests but we see him more often than the real owner.

Monsieur Baroth has invited us to dinner because the real owner, his wife, Pierrette Girard, is coming to spend a couple of weeks in her maison troglodytes. I have often wondered why she doesn't come more often, but I know that Monsieur Baroth comes for the seclusion that is necessary for all artists to think and create. We soon learn that Pierrette is a writer as well as a psychiatrist. Aprille is delighted that she can talk with someone about Freudian versus Jungian psychiatry, art, literature and whatever. But I am interested in the caves.

As it turns out Chateau Chèvre is more cave than chateau. Some homes are built up against the cliff face with a small cave in the rear but Chateau Chèvre is a series of caves that go deep into the mountain. The facade and the one building constructed in front make it is look like a normal house. There is a fireplace and old dark portraits of serious men whose eyes follow you everywhere you go in the room. Baroth, as Pierrette calls him, offers us a tour of the house. The house part is on the facade. The rest is a series of caves, galleries and chambers that connect to other caves on the goat path. One of the chambers is bricked up. Baroth explained that it is a tunnel that goes for miles into the mountain and exits somewhere down by Chateau Lavardin. When I asked why it is bricked up, Baroth laughs and says it is for security.

There is a set of wooden stairs in front of the bricked up gallery that leads to the only building that is not a cave. Upstairs is a bedroom and downstairs is the library with more of the dark, foreboding portraits. Baroth explains that the portraits where done by students of an artist who lived here in the 1940's.

One cave has a bunch of old plaster sculptures, moldy paintings and unfinished canvases. Baroth explains that the former owner was an artist who died here after a long-suffering illness that left him paralyzed. His wife left immediately after he died without taking anything with her. The property was left abandoned for a long time and even the vandals and thieves left it alone after one break-in.

When we return to the dining room, Baroth points to a corner of the room and says that was where the artist, Jean Bailleul, spent the last days of his life. I remember that I had seen this man's grave in the village cemetery.

I remember it because it was broken open. When I volunteer this information, Pierrette and Baroth look at each other but don't say anything.

I ask Pierrette why the tunnel was bricked up but it is Baroth who answers. He often sleeps in the library that can now only be entered from the courtyard. The door to the library from the caves was sealed because he kept hearing noises like someone walking up the stairs and trying the door latch. Pierrette interrupts and says that she lent the house to a friend who stayed in the bedroom upstairs and was terrified by the same type noises. She was so afraid that she moved to a house down the hill near the château. But the next night she heard the same noises. It turns out that the tunnel is connected to the caves near that house. So they bricked up the tunnel.

Baroth tells us that the tunnel goes for miles back into the mountain and nobody knows where all the different galleries exit. He suggests that a thief could get in the house if he could find one of those entrances. I jokingly ask if any of the tunnels go in the direction of the cemetery. After an awkward silence, he tells me they go everywhere.

Aprille senses the tension and tries to change the subject to art. She asks why all those old canvases are left in that moldy cave. She likes some of the work and is interested in the restoration of old paintings. Baroth says that it all has to stay where it is. Our importuning silence demands an answer. Finally Pierrette explains that she consulted a colleague about the possibility of the ghost of Jean Bailleul being in her caves. Her colleague suggested that she treat it like a patient and counsel it to cross over to the other world. Pierrette went into the caves and told whatever or whoever was there to not be afraid of crossing over to the other world and that it was time to go.

They bricked up the tunnel and they have not heard the noises for years. They decided to leave the paintings and canvases where they are and the tunnel will remain bricked up.

As Aprille and I are walking home, I ask what she thinks of this ghost stuff. She says, "I don't believe a word of it," and I think, "Yeah, me too. But I am glad there are no tunnels leading to our cave."

Cult Of The Black Virgin

Except for a few little near death experiences when I was praying like a saint, I have never taken religion very seriously. I can recall sitting on the front row at the Saint Simons Methodist Church with my best friend, Jack Marshall, when I was five years old. We went to Sunday school every Sunday but once a month our parents let us sit together during communion. I don't know why they made this same mistake over and over again because we always had to be separated and forced to sit with the rest of the family at some time during the middle of the service. It was the communion ceremony that always caused the problem. As soon as the preacher started talking about eating flesh and drinking blood, we would howl with laughter. I still see parents taking their children to church and I wonder why parents expect children to understand the complex symbolism of Christianity.

In the south where I grew up, the complex symbolism is not so important. It boils down to a simple rule: "Accept Jesus Christ as your Lord and Savior and you will be saved". There is really not much more to it. But in Europe, it is a different story. The history of Christianity here goes back two thousand years and there is a mythology surrounding it that rivals the Greeks and Romans. There are pilgrimages, cults, holy relics, secret societies, Knights Templar, crusades, martyrs, saints and the Holy Grail.

Probably the most fascinating of these mysteries is the cult of the black virgin. There are 210 black virgin sculptures in various churches and chapels around France. They are mostly in the south, with the largest concentration in the Auvergne region. The origins of these statutes are almost always mysterious. When I heard that there was a black virgin sculpture in the neighboring village of Villavard and that an annual pilgrimage from Lavardin takes place each year, I wanted to take part in it.

There are some unfounded legends concerning the origin of this black virgin but the real story is more interesting than the legends. According to *Le livre des miracles de Chartres* (Book of Miracles of Chartres), the black virgin of Villavard is a copy of the black virgin of Chartres. In the eleventh century, Villavard was a commune of Lavardin and the Lord of Montoire coveted its rich plain. During one of the battles for this plain, the Lord of Lavardin lost the reins of his horse and was captured. As he was being led off, the bridle came off his horse and he spurred it to escape. The horse bolted toward the Loir River where he faced certain death by drowning in full armor. As the horse approached the river he prayed to the black virgin of Chartres for salvation. The horse suddenly turned at the bank of the river and he was saved not only from drowning but also from being captured. He was so moved by this experience that he made a vow to visit the Virgin's shrine in Chartres. When he returned from Chartres, he built a church near the place of combat and placed therein a copy of the black virgin of Chartres. Such is the origin of the black virgin of Villavard.

It is only two miles from Lavardin to Villavard but pilgrimage participation in the past few years has been low. Last year there were only about five people who walked. Many of these small pilgrimages throughout Europe have already disappeared but there is hope for this one. The young Priest leading this procession has recruited the local scouts to participate, so we are easily thirty or forty penitent sinners singing *Ave Maria* and trudging along in the rain. The procession follows a small sculpture of the virgin that is hoisted on a litter carried by two young scouts. The procession stops at a small wayside sculpture of the virgin at the town limits of Lavardin. The priest gives a prayer and the singing recommences as the procession climbs the hillside leading to Villavard. The group stops again near an old Templar *commanderie* where we sing and give prayers.

As we approach the church, I am beginning to feel a little out of place. I am not Catholic and don't really understand the ceremony of this church. It is not the scouts that make me nervous. It is the handful of octogenarians who have made the march while fingering rosaries and mumbling prayers. This is serious business for a few faithful and I feel as if I am interfering. As we approach the door of the church, I consider leaving but I still have not seen the black virgin and it is raining. As I enter the church, my thoughts are of Jack Marshall and how thankful I am that he is not here. If they start eating flesh and drinking blood, it will be in French and I will probably miss the translation.

When we enter the church, I see the black virgin on the left high up on an alter. It is very black and very impressive. Perhaps it is the formality of the ceremony or just the drama of discovery, but I am moved by this spectacle. I know that it is at least one thousand years old and that it is a copy of a sculpture more than two thousand years old.

There is something in the sheer numbers that evokes an emotion. The original black virgin of Chartres predated the birth of Christ by several hundred years making it the most mysterious of all of them. It was made by druids who predicted the coming of Christ two hundred years before his birth. The sculpture was placed in a kind of chapel dug into a grotto. It was above this grotto that the first cathedral of Chartres was built. This subterranean chapel eventually became the crypt of the cathedral.

The druids had received a revelation of the coming of a new order in which a virgin would bear a child. After receiving this revelation, they dug the subterranean chapel and placed the wooden statue representing the virgin and child inside. The underground chapel was a symbol of the night, which in turn was a symbol of the wait for the birth of a Savior. It was in this chapel that Aymeric Aymard, the lord of Lavardin, came nine hundred years ago to thank the Madonna for having saved him from captivity and death. My next pilgrimage will be to Chartres.

Pot-au-Feu à l'Ancienne

One of the traditional dishes of cave dwellers in the French countryside is *pot-au-feu*. *Pot-au-feu* means pot in the fire and that describes how this dish was prepared in the old days. The ingredients are placed in a cast iron or clay pot and placed directly in the fire to simmer for several hours. I sometimes prepare this dish just to smell the aromas while skinning animals and drawing bisons on the walls. Here is how it is made.

Pot-au-Feu

Ingredients:
3 pounds of beef
4 liters of water
Gray sea salt
4 carrots
1 parsnip
1 turnip
4 leeks tied together
1 branch of celery
1 branch of thyme
1 branch of parsley
1 onion

Directions:
While the fire is making hot coals, place three pounds of beef in your clay or cast iron pot. The cuts of beef can be rump, round (topside), top rump, rib roast or chuck steak. Add four liters of cold water to the pot and add a handful of gray sea salt. Place the pot uncovered in front of the fire. When a white foam (fat) appears on the surface of the water, dip it out with a spoon until it

is all gone. After all the foam is removed, add four carrots, one parsnip, one turnip, four leeks tied together, one branch of celery, one branch of thyme and one branch of parsley. Finally add one onion that has already been cooked in the coals or caramelized in the oven. Cover and simmer in the fire for six hours. Place crusts of bread or toast in large soup bowls and serve the pot-au-feu over the bread.

If you are still a little hungry try this simple recipe while the fire is still burning:

Pommes de Terre aux Lard
(Potatoes cooked with Bacon)

Ingredients:
Potatoes
Onions
Thick Slices of Bacon
Directions:
Cover the bottom of your cast iron pot with strips of smoked bacon. Cover the bacon with slices of potatoes. Cover the potatoes with slices of onions. Put a large whole onion in the center of the pot and continue to fill the pot with layers of potatoes and onions. Finish by putting another layer of smoked bacon over the top. Cover and cook slowly for three or four hours.

Here is another recipe for any potatoes and onions left over. This is a true traditional recipe of the Savoie region of France and is the answer to that nagging weight loss problem some of us experience. My friend, Christine Montambaux, invited us for Tartiflette one cold winter evening and gave me this recipe.

La Tartiflette

Ingredients:
400 grams of potatoes per person

Onions
Bacon cut in cubes
Roblochon cheese
Lard
Directions:
   Peel and wash the potatoes; slice each potato in thin slices and wash again; brown the bacon cubes in the lard. Add the slices of potatoes and onions and cook until brown. Add according to taste fresh herbs, salt and pepper. Cover with slices of Reblochon cheese and allow to brown at medium temperature for about 40 minutes. When the aromas of the cheese, potatoes, bacon and onions melt together, it is ready to be served.

Pigs I

November is traditionally the month for slaughtering pigs on the small family farms in France. It is usually cool enough in November to complete the three days of hard work without spoiling the meat. Although it is a rare event today, the tradition still exists and the pig remains an important part of the French diet. Of course modern farms are no longer constrained by the weather or tradition, but butchering a pig was a common occurrence on small family farms just a few years ago. I witnessed the slaughter of a pig on my grandmother's farm fifty years ago and although I was only five years old, I can still remember my father and his six brothers and sisters working all day long in pools of blood and guts. It was very impressive and many *campagnards* of the Loir Valley remember how it is done.

The pig has always been an important weapon against famine and starvation in Europe. Absolutely nothing is wasted. Everything is eaten. That thirty-pound *porcelet* purchased in April now weights three hundred pounds and is ready for slaughter. At the turn of the last century, the aid of a *segnur* (pig butchering expert) or *charcutier spécialiste* was necessary but the whole family was usually necessary for the job.

Segnurs are hard to find nowadays, so I did a little research to find out how it is accomplished. Monsieur Jean arranged a visit to the pig farm of Gilles Capps near the village of Houssay. Gilles tells me that modern farms no longer kill and butcher their pigs. They are all sent off to an *abattoir* (slaughter house) in Clermont-Ferrand for processing. However, I met a donkey named Mr. Ed who knew a lot about the subject. When I approached the donkey to take his picture, he commenced to sing something that sounded like the Marseillaise. He didn't stop until I left. The pigs were less colorful but more poignant. After five minutes in the building where they are kept before that big truck ride to Clermont-Ferrand, my cloths were completely impregnated with the smell of pig shit. Jean and I were pursued by packs of dogs all day long as we traversed the valley in search of a *segnur*. All of my clothes had to be washed but it was all worth the trouble. I learned how to butcher a pig. Here are the instructions:

Attach the pig's right rear hoof (or whatever a pig has at the end of its legs) with a cord. Use another cord to tie the upper jaw of the pig to your ankle. Tighten the cord so its head does not move. This allows the animal to squeal a long time when its throat is cut. Squealing speeds the bleeding.

When the pig is tied and secured, make two cuts in a V shape in its throat. Empty the blood into buckets. Pour the buckets of blood into a larger vessel where one member of the family should begin to stir the warm blood by hand to prevent it from clotting. The blood will be used for making sausages later.

Stretch the carcass out on a bed of straw. Cover it with another layer of straw and set it on fire to burn off the fur. After burning off all the fur, scrape the skin with tiles or the edge of a knife. Wash the scraped skin with clean water.

Remove the testicles by a quick twisting, snatching movement. Wipe the cold sweat from your brow.

With a sharp knife, make a long slice the length of the stomach and chest until the innards are revealed. The French argot for these innards are *la boufie, les rognons, le chodin, la coeffe, la pire dure* and *la pire molle. La boufie* is the stomach, *les rognons* are the kidneys and *la coeffe* is the heart, lungs and spleen. The rest are just parts.

Pull out the entire contents of the cavity and separate them with care. Use a hatchet to break the spinal column from top to bottom. Distribute the various innards to the family members. The stomach (*la boufie*) when dried and inflated makes a great balloon for the children. The tail is usually given to a young woman in the family and everyone makes phallic jokes about it.

The next day fires are built and ovens are heated. The heavily larded meat is simmered all day to make *rillettes, rilles, rolets* and *pâtés*. Part of the *coeffe* is used to cover the *pâtés*. The blood and intestines are used to make blood sausage (*boudin noir*). The intestines are also used to make another type sausage with the *couane* and the *viande moulue*. I believe these sausages are called *andouilles*.

The best parts of the pig are the hams that are rubbed with eau-de-vie, covered with salt and pepper, and wrapped in a type of rough cloth. After ten or fifteen days they are hung high in the chimney for smoking.

The third day is dedicated to making *fressure. Fressure* is the meat not yet used which includes the heart, liver, spleen and lungs. It is simmered all day long in a large cauldron with bread and onions. At the end of the evening blood and a broth of milk and flour are added. I believe this is consumed like soup.

Lard, rillettes and *rillons* are stored in ceramic pots called *saloirs*. Salt is used for conservation. *Andouilles* are hung in the kitchen to dry in winter but in the summer they are also stored in brine in a *saloir*. The roasts, pates, and blood sausage are consumed immediately. One pig could feed a family for several months.

Pig II

The pig story was so popular that I have to do a follow-up. I am a little surprised that so many people have witnessed a pig slaughter. It seems that many Americans remember it, like me, from their youth. For others who worked on farms it was hard work and not a pleasant memory. My French friends remember it quite differently. For them it is a pleasant memory of celebration, family and fellowship.

Here is a translation of a letter that I received from Pierre and Claude Chêne who grew up in the French countryside west of Bordeaux:

Chers Amis,

Your last email on the subject surrounding the traditions of the pig takes our memories back more than fifty years. We have a little to add on the subject of the *boudin noir* (blood sausage).

In the Gironde and the Dordogne (perhaps elsewhere), a ceremony existed on the day of the cooking of the *boudin*. It was a true ritual. On the third morning, the women cleaned vast quantities of leeks, carrots and turnips. The men prepared the wood to feed the fires under large cast iron pots in the fireplace. Then everyone would spread out through the village to invite all of the other families to come precisely at six or seven o'clock in the evening to share the *gimbourra* (the vegetable soup created from making blood sausage). In effect, the cooking of the blood sausage was done by soaking several meters of the sausages in the soup of vegetables. The sausages were divided into sections by tying strips of wicker at intervals. It was a true art because if the sausage touched the edge of the hot pot, it would explode. (I hate it when that happens). There was always someone who accidentally dropped his knife in the soup and that was okay because it added to the taste of the soup.

As soon as the sausages were cooked, they were carefully laid in a large wicker basket covered with linen cloth. The whole basket was also carefully covered to insure that the sausage cooled slowly during the night. The next day the sausages were stretched on strings in the attic to dry. When the *boyau* (the intestines used to hold the sausage together) dried, what a delicious treat during the winter months. Just put them on the grilled with a little butter.

At the precise hour of the invitation, the neighbors would arrive to form a line for a taste of the soup. The smells of the cooking sausage put everyone in a good humor. My grandparents would usually slip a pork chop or sausage in the baskets of the older people, especially those living alone. Nostalgia…? Yeah, but these simple moments of rejoicing brought so much warmth and happiness.

Even if there is no *gimbourra* in your marmite, I hope that the fire in your hearth will warm you.

Claude Chêne

(a/k/a La Dame de Moulin de Beaumé)

Pigs III

First there was Rocky IV, then Rambo XI, and now Pigs III will squeeze the last breath of life from this subject. I was invited to a pig killing at one of the local farms. It is the tradition of holding back a pig for the family that interests me and not the carnage of the kill so I have decided not to show any photographs. Local farmer Raymond Gillard decided to hire a *charcutier* to kill his pig and turn it into food. The *charcutier* arrived with a truck full of tools and instruments to complete the job. Many of the tools are the same as those used a hundred years ago. Others are modern and make it possible to complete a three-day job in nine hours.

As in days of yore, one of the hind legs of the pig is attached to a wall, which remarkably immobilizes the animal. The *charcutier* uses something like the bang sticks used by divers for killing sharks to kill the pig. He immediately cuts the throat and gathers the blood in a bucket that he constantly stirs to keep it from clotting. After about ten minutes, he stops stirring and sets the bucket aside. Evidently, it is only necessary to stir the blood for a short time to keep it from coagulating.

The dead pig is dragged into the courtyard to burn the fur off. Instead of firing straw as in the old days, the *charcutier* uses a butane torch that leaves the pig looking like a Fourth of July hot dog (black). Instead of scraping the pig with tiles, he uses a high-pressure hose that leaves the pig immaculately white.

The pig is placed on its back on a litter and cut open. All of the guts are taken out and cleaned for making sausage. *Andouillettes* will never taste the same. The cleaning of the intestines was the most time consuming part of the process. The meat was cut into quarters and laid out on a table to set for the night. It is cool enough so that it will not spoil. The hams and sausages will be smoked. The fatty parts will be simmered for hours the next day to make *rillettes, rillons* and whatever.

As usual in the *bas vendômois*, we celebrate the end of the job with a glass or two of *pousse d'épine*. Actually, this part of the ceremony takes place every day. Oh! It's raining. Let's drink to the rain. Oh! Its Monday…Let's have another. And so life goes on today as *d'antan* (the old days).

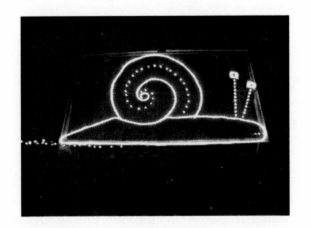

Winter

Most people don't realize that France is on the same latitude as Canada. Although the winters in France are much milder than those in Canada, the length of the days and nights is the same. It is dark all winter. Night falls at five o'clock in the evening and daylight returns about nine o'clock the next day. If it is raining, it seems like daylight never arrives. It could be a depressing environment but it is not. It is the holidays and a time of celebration. The Christmas season is celebrated from the beginning of December through the end of January and the people of the Loir Valley compensate for the short, dark days with dinners, dances and parties that last all night long.

The first celebrations of winter are the village Christmas markets that are held during the first two weeks of December. Although a few Christmas ornaments are sold at these markets, the emphasis is on food. Wine merchants sell glasses of sauvignon at *buvettes* set up next to stands selling oysters. Hot spiced wine is sold with *cornets* of hot roasted chestnuts. Grilled sausage is sold with *barquettes* of French fries and coffee is served with crêpes and galettes. Lavardin's Christmas market takes place during the first week of December and it represents a deadline for putting up Christmas lights and decorations. Christmas lights on medieval buildings give the season a special authenticity. There is a friendly competition among the villages for the best decorations and hundreds of people stroll through markets to eat, drink and enjoy the season.

Winter is the time of year for eating those hearty dishes that were traditionally cooked over the fire. Although not so many people still cook them over the fire, in the Loir Valley many still use their fireplaces for the traditional dishes. *Pot-au-feu, tartiflette, lards aux pommes de terre*, and *choucroute* are normal fare for the evening meals.

The celebration of Christmas lasts until the day of Epiphany. These are the twelve days of Christmas that were traditionally marked by the burning of a large Yule log that lasted twelve days. Today, the Yule log has been replaced by a cake shaped like a log that is eaten during the season. On Christmas day and New Yeas day, families celebrate with a large meal that includes oysters, *fruits de mer*, Champagne, and an endless train of courses that last late into the night. The meal on New Year's day is the same and often bigger.

The final day of the Christmas season is the *fêtes des rois* or Epiphany. It is celebrated on the sixth of January with the consumption of galettes and Champagne. In the Loir Valley this celebration is extended up until the end of January although a *vin petillant* from Vouvray is often substituted for the Champagne.

On January 23, the winter season is capped with the festival of Saint Vincent. This is the festival of the wine growers and at one time, they paid for paid for everything. Today, everyone contributes and participates but the celebration is the same. There is a long meal that lasts into the night with toasts, singing and dancing. A second meal with onion soup finishes the evening. The wine is always copious.

February is quiet. It is a time to rest and relax because spring is just around the corner.

Back to France

We are heading back to our cave in Lavardin after a month of traveling and visiting family in the States. The eight-hour flight from Atlanta to Paris almost seems routine now. It is still a long sleepless night that leaves us sick with the fatigue of *décalage horaire,* but the French accents and the food on our Air France flight remind us of where we are going.

Although the flight arrived at six o'clock in the morning, we don't get back to Lavardin until two o'clock in the afternoon. The TGV (*Train à Grande Vitesse*) from Gare Montparnasse in Paris to Vendôme only takes forty-two minutes, but the speed seems irrelevant when you have to wait four hours to leave the station.

We try to stay awake to get back on French time but it is hopeless. I fall asleep, but within an hour I hear a knock on the door. Maurice Cheron saw my car at the foot of the mountain and decided to come up and tell me the good news. He tells me that he has just purchased forty-three liters

161

of a very good Bordeaux for me and that it needs to be bottled soon. He hands me the corks and labels. I tell him that I will come down later. I try to go back to sleep but I keep thinking of that dark, rich red liquid losing its essence in a plastic container. I get up and go down to see Maurice.

He is in the process of loading apples in a large bin. I ask him if he is making *eau-de-vie* but he tells me the apples are for cider. He owns a half dozen caves that are all dedicated to the production and preservation of alcohol in one form or another. Last year he was making *eau-de-vie* from apples. He uses the *eau-de-vie* to make *pousse d'épine*, *feuille de pêcher* and *vin côt*. Maurice is about sixty-five years old and seems to have limitless energy, most of which is spent in the production of alcoholic beverages. All I have to do is ask how one makes cider to get the full course.

Cider is made very much like wine. The apples are crushed and pressed to get the juice out. The juice goes from a vat to barrels where it is allowed to ferment. As the dregs settle to the bottom, the top portion of the juice is drawn off into another barrel. This process is repeated four times about one month apart. The result is apple cider, which normally has an alcohol content of about 3% or 4%. When Maurice tells me that his cider has an alcohol content of 8%, I raise an eyebrow in disbelief. He catches my expression and tells me that he adds a little sugar to raise the alcohol content. No self-respecting man would drink a beverage with less than 8% alcohol.

I am ready to get down to the business of my Bordeaux, but no business transaction in the *bas vendômois* can proceed without a taste of something to relax the tension of a transfer of money. Maurice pours me a *pousse d'épine* and I admire the dark rich color before sipping this spicy, port-tasting liquid. I tell him that the *pousse d'épine* that I made in July has turned a cloudy brown color. He tells me that my problem is that I let myself be guided by the counsels of Monsieur Jean who is much better at drinking *pousse d'épine* than making it. Of course Jean and Maurice are old friends and never miss a chance to dig at each other a little. Nevertheless, I include myself among the group who drink better than fabricate, so I write down the advice of Maurice which is to let *les épines* leaves steep longer in the *eau-de-vie* before adding the wine and use a sealed container so the gases won't escape. It just goes to show that even the most serious problems in life have a solution.

Maurice finally gives me the bill for the thirty-two liters of Bordeaux. He says that 768 francs is a lot to pay for thirty-two liters but that this is a very good Bordeaux that has been aging in the barrel since 1998. He tells me thirty-two liters will make forty-three bottles and that Monsieur Jean will find me some Bordeaux bottles, which are *de rigueur* for Bordeaux wine. I do a quick calculation to estimate the cost of this precious liquid. It is about $2.40 per bottle. I love this country.

Miranda This

Much to the consternation of French policemen, a common scene is occurring more and more in France. Local gendarmes stop a man to check his vehicle registration. The indignant Frenchman demands his Miranda rights and a lawyer for his defense. When he is informed that he does not have these rights, he is outraged. He knows the law by heart.

> *You have the right to remain silent. Anything you say can and will be used against you in a court of law. You have the right to an attorney. If you can't afford an attorney, one will be provided…*

Of course every American knows it by heart too. Its on television every night and practically every movie quotes it. But why do the French think they have Miranda rights?

There is a whole generation of French who grew up watching Kojak, Columbo and hundreds of other American programs and movies where policemen speaking French read suspects their Miranda rights. Since American television programs and films are dubbed in French, the viewers assume that the programs and films are taking place in France.

Most Americans are opposed to mollycoddling criminals with things like Miranda rights and somehow it does seem unpatriotic. Everybody ought to cooperate with the police, but recent events have shown that Americans will confess to anything even if they are innocent. All it takes is for a policeman to say "You know that it will go easier on you if you confess" to get someone to confess that he shot Lincoln from a grassy knoll in Dallas.

The student living in the hotel next to the World Trade Center confessed three times to being involved in the attacks although he was completely innocent. Of course he was kept in solitary confinement for a month, which is something akin to torture, but, in general, confessions come easy and the confessors are very often innocent. Policemen tell me that people blurt out confessions before they have a chance to ask them their names. Next to eyewitness identification, confessions are becoming the most unreliable evidence presented in courtrooms.

But false confessions are not a problem in France. The French know they have a right to remain silent and don't have to say anything until they are provided an attorney. America has swamped France with its cultural exports. American movies, music, T-shirts and fast-food are everywhere. Now we can add Miranda to the list.

Thanksgiving

Food is a very serious subject in France and everyone here is a kind of expert on the subject. This is common knowledge to anyone who has traveled in France but few know the extent to which food is studied by the academics. I went to Blois to see what was going on with an exposition that I had seen advertised in the paper. It was called *Nourritures Terrestres* and was three days of seminars, conferences, debates, demonstrations and a replica of an ancient market. It was basically a three-day conference on the subject of food and wine. However the lectures were not what you might ordinarily expect to hear at a conference on food and wine. There were no chefs speaking on subjects like the best way to make *crème brûlée* or wine experts talking about legs, nose or bouquet. These speakers were all university professors who were speaking about history, culture and the anthropological significance of food and drink. The seminars started mid-morning and lasted until ten o'clock at night and there were three or four different seminars going on at the same time. If you wanted to hear the seminar on the subject of "Absinthe under the Third Republic", you might have to miss the seminar on "Food and Colonization." Examples of other titles are "Do the people of Provence really like olive oil?", "Food for travel in the 19th Century", "Jewish Food in Provence in the Middle Ages", "Famines of yesterday and today", etc. When I arrived at the Conference Hall, I had a choice between the lectures on "Chocolate from the seventeenth to the nineteenth century", "Funeral Meals in Savoie in the Middle Ages" and "American Thanksgiving." I really wanted to hear the other two lectures but I could not pass up the chance to hear what the French thought of our Thanksgiving celebration.

The seminar was presented by a scholar name Monsieur Bernard Sinsheimer who spoke slowly and clearly so I understood most of what he was saying. He started by describing the Thanksgiving holiday as a festival of fat that is unique in American culture not because of the fatty food but more so because it is a holiday uniquely revered by Americans. He first described how Americans generally have little respect for their holidays. He said Americans would take a holiday like a former President' s birthday and move it to a day that is more convenient like a Monday so that everybody can have a long weekend. Or even worse, Americans might combine all the birthdays of their presidents into one day that is convenient and have only one celebration.

His point was that Americans don't revere the day or the event as much as the long weekend off from work. He said that it is this general lack of respect that makes the Thanksgiving celebration so unique. Thanksgiving is devoutly and universally revered in America. It is always celebrated on the fourth Thursday in November even though Friday is a workday for many Americans.

In addition to this unique respect that Americans have for Thanksgiving, he also pointed out that it is the one day of the year where American families gather even from great distances to be together, and everyone, regardless of race, religion or creed, celebrates it. The professor also went into some detail about our unusual eating habits and he describe the traditional dishes like sweet potatoes, squash, corn, pumpkin pie, stuffing in the turkey and giblet gravy.

However, the thing that brought gasps of surprise to this small but intensely interested audience was his description of placing the whole turkey on the table and someone trying to carve it in front of everyone waiting to eat. I don't really understand why carving the turkey on the table was such a horrendous idea but it seemed to draw excited murmurs from our group.

An even stronger reaction came from his description of what we drink with our Thanksgiving meal. He said wine is rare but growing in popularity.

Of course this alone is enough to convince the French of our savagery, but for those not yet convinced, the *coup de grâce* was the revelation that we drink iced tea and even Coca Cola with the meal. After revealing this horror to us he said after a dramatic pause "Some people even drink coffee with the meal." The words "*Quel horreur!*" pealed from the audience.

The audience was intensely interested in the American Thanksgiving feast and many told stories of their experiences in America and how much they liked the food, especially the oyster stuffing from New England. Others talked of the pumpkin pie and sweet potatoes with marshmallows on top. However the most humorous thing that I heard was the description of everybody falling asleep after dinner watching a football game.

I asked Professor Sinsheimer for a copy of his lecture but he only had hand written notes and did not think the lecture would be printed. I was fascinated and amused to hear this description of America from the French point of view. The lecture also gave me a better understanding of why my French friends are so fascinated by my observations of their habits and customs. It is one of those things where you say, "Yeah, that's true but I just never thought about it like that."

Table Etiquette

French restaurants can be intimidating for Americans who are less formal in their approach to eating. Most restaurants in France put an array of glasses, plates and utensils on the table that can baffle the most sophisticated visitors. There is usually an elegant plate with an artistically folded linen napkin in the center. Above the plat are four wine glasses of various shapes and sizes. There are three forks and sometimes a large spoon on the left side, two knives on the right and a spoon and maybe a small fork at the top of the plate. Bread is usually placed on the table but sometimes there is a small plate for it.

The largest glass is usually for water and the white wine glass is larger that the red wine glass. If you order a wine from the Burgundy region of France a large bowl shaped glass will be provided. Forks are on the left and knives are on the right. Use the ones on the outside and work your way toward the middle. If fish is being served, there will be a special knife and fork for this course. They are a little shorter and wider than the other utensils. If soup is on the menu, a soupspoon will be on the left.

The French eat with the fork in the left hand and cut with the knife in the right hand. I have never been quite sure what you do with the knife and fork between bites. They have to be placed on the plate, but this is some times awkward and I have seen the French do this in so many different ways that I am not sure what is correct. The waiter will come by between courses and scrape up the bread crumbs, so don't worry about the tablecloth.

In the homes and small restaurants in the countryside of France, etiquette is much simpler. A fork, a knife, a plate and one glass usually suffices at the family dinner table. The custom is to clean the plate and utensils after each course with bread, but a clean plate and fork is usually provided for dessert. Even though the etiquette is simple, the meals are served in courses as in restaurants and you are expected to finish everything on your plate. In restaurants as well as in homes, bread should be broken off in small bite size pieces with your hands. It is more common to use bread to sop up the sauces left on the plate at home than it is in the restaurants, but I see the French do it all the time and they are expert in hiding this maneuver. It is probably best not to do it in the very fine restaurants.

It all seems very complicated and the rules change with different menus. There are special instruments for snails and something like *bouillabaisse* requires a course in physics. I still have trouble discerning the difference between the white wine glass and the water glass but I am learning that the important thing is not to be intimidated by a waiter. If you want to snort a line of *coulis* with a straw, the waiter should accept it. I learned this while traveling with a group of elderly retired people from a neighboring village.

When the waiter arrived with the first course everyone started eating with the wrong fork. The first course was a seafood pastry that should be eaten with the fish fork and fish knife. Everyone was using the larger meat fork and knife. When the waiter returned he was thoroughly disgusted and looking in the air in exasperation. Some of the people discerned their mistake and tried to put the clean fish fork on the plate. This made matters worse because the menu had two fish courses and we were supposed to keep the fish utensils for the second course. By the time the second fish course arrived, knives and forks of every description were everywhere. To make matters worse, everyone was balling up their napkins and putting them on the table where the plates had just been taken away. The waiter was pushing napkins out of the way, straightening the array of forks and scolding everybody's grandmother for their table manners. We were not in Paris, but this waiter had taken on the airs of the big city. He was doomed to frustration because absolutely no one paid any attention to him.

You can ignore the waiter but not the ceremony. It is quasi-religious in France: Aperitif, *amuses bouches, entrée, plat principal, fromage, dessert, café* and *digestif.* You can omit as many courses as you like but never mess with the order of consumption. For the last three years, we have been requesting that coffee be served with the dessert. Our requests have never been honored. I dread the day that it finally happens. I like things the way they are.

Let Them Eat Cake

I once saw a Far Side cartoon that showed Marie-Antoinette on the scaffold leading to the guillotine trying to explain to the mob that what she really said was "Let them eat cake AND ice cream." But bread is no joking matter in France. Perhaps it lacks the glamour of wine but it is more basic and necessary to the French soul than any other product. Although bread has been around for a long time, it was in the eighteenth century that it became really popular. It was the development of *forment*, a soft fine wheat, that made bread so popular with the people. Many people believe that it was the popularity and subsequent scarcity of bread that led to the French Revolution. In the early part of the eighteenth century, the bakers in France started forming corporations to standardize the process and sale of bread. One of these corporations became large enough to create a monopoly and manipulate the price of wheat. Bread became so expensive, that only the aristocracy could afford it. When the people started complaining, someone in Marie-Antoinette's circle made the famous statement: *"Ils n'ont plus de pain, qu'ils mangent de la brioche"* (Let them eat cake). No matter who actually uttered these words, they are today attributed to Marie-Antoinette and are a symbol of the perceived attitude of the aristocracy toward the people. In the following years of the revolution, mobs routinely attacked, killed and dismembered bakers and others deemed responsible for the lack of bread.

The terror was so great during these years that the National Assembly banned the corporations and began regulating the production of bread. Even today the production and sale of bread is strictly regulated. The price of bread is the same in every bakery in France. The only exception to the standardized price is when an artisan does something special like kneading by hand or baking in an ancient oven with wood. However, every deviation in price must be strictly justified.

The village baker in Lavardin told me last summer that he would spend a day with me and show me how to make bread when things slowed down a little. When we got back to France last week, Philippe Débrée, the *boulanger*, told Aprille and me to show up at 5:00 a.m. on Friday for our lesson. In the winter when business is slow, he starts his working day at 5:00 a.m. In the busy season, he starts at 3:00 a.m. Philippe explained that he generally works up to about noon. After lunch he might take a short nap but most of the time he is too busy to rest. He goes to bed early, so there is not much leisure time for the *boulangers* in France. He jokes that French bakers hardly have any time to see their wives and have to contract with the *facteurs* (postmen) if they want to have children.

We start with a quick tour of the building. Philippe rents the boulangerie and the three-room apartment above. Like most buildings in Lavardin, it is very old. It is a sixteenth century structure with large wooden beams and mortar on the outside facade. Inside, there is a shop where customers come to buy bread and pastries, a room for baking *(le fournil*) and a room for making the *pâtisseries (la pâtisserie or laboratoire)* There is also a small kitchen on the ground floor which is a part of the upstairs apartment. We begin our day in the baking room that Philippe calls the *fournil*. This room contains an oven and a large locker for controlling the fermentation of the bread.

The oven is important but it is the fermentation locker that the baker loves best. Bread is made with flour, water, salt and yeast. It is a very simple and healthy concoction. After the ingredients are mixed and kneaded, it is normally necessary to wait about five to six hours for the bread to ferment (rise). Fermentation depends on the temperature and humidity. The fermentation locker gives the baker some control over the time of fermentation. Otherwise, the baker would have to work all night to make his *pâte* (dough) and bake the bread for his seven o'clock customers. It would be a very hard life without the fermentation locker.

Philippe begins by placing *croissants* and *pains au chocolat* in one of the four baking chambers. We retire to the kitchen to take a *petit café* and I notice that Philippe does not use a *minuterie* (timer). He says that he has one, but he just keeps time in his head. This seems to work fairly well because, after about twenty minutes, he suddenly jumps up and says it is time to check the *croissants*. We go to the *fournil* and pull out the golden brown *croissants* and *pains au chocolat*.

Now it is time to start baking the bread. The uncooked bread that we are pulling out of the fermentation locker this morning was actually made two days ago. It is stacked on rippled canvas sheets on rolling shelves. The canvas is wet from the fermentation process. Philippe has already warmed up the oven so the bread is ready for baking. When he opens an oven door to check the temperature, steam screams out of the front. He explains that the steam is very important because it suppresses the carbonic gases that escape from the fermented bread as it cooks. The lack of this feature in household ovens makes it very difficult to make this kind of bread at home. Philippe lines the *ficelles* and *baguettes* on a long, manual conveyor belt in rows of ten. He takes a razor blade and slices long diagonal lines across the top of each piece of bread. He lets Aprille and me try the cutting, but we are way too slow, so he finishes the work. He explains that the slices are important to let the gases escape from the bread. He slides the bread into each of the four long chambers and the baking commences. It takes about twenty minutes for each batch and Philippe continues to keep time in his head. I am trying to take pictures but the light is low and Philippe is in constant motion even when we are waiting for the bread to bake. We are constantly running between the *fournil* and the *pâtisserie* to take advantage of every minute. All of my pictures are blurred from the motion.

After about twenty minutes, we head back to the *fournil* to take out the first batch of bread. The sound is incredible. It is cracking and popping from the escaping gas and the room fills with the aroma of warm, fresh bread. He explains that this is a very slow time of the year and so he is only making 230 *baguettes*, 100 *pains* and a couple dozen *ficelles*. He is also baking some *pain de compagne* and some *pain rond*. Since the population of Lavardin is only about 250 people, this seems like a lot of bread. He explains that he also sells to some surrounding farms. The baking takes about three hours. Philippe pours us a glass of wine to celebrate the success. I hardly blink at an eight o'clock *coup* nowadays. It seems quite natural.

I ask when he makes the *pâte* for tomorrow's bread and he tells me that he normally begins immediately after baking the bread but he is out of flour. He is waiting for the arrival of the *meunier* (miller). His flour is delivered about once a month and stored in a large container in the attic. The flour pours down a round flexible duct into a huge vat for mixing. Philippe adds water, yeast and salt to the flour and a giant mixer kneads the dough. When the miller arrives and fills his container from a large truck, he finishes the *pâte* and lets it rest for fifteen minutes. Then he weighs out equal amounts of the *pâte* and places each batch in a machine that divides it precisely. He explains that there is a significant fine if each *baguette* and *pain* is not exactly the weight required by law. The specter of the Revolution still hangs over France.

The carefully cut batches are rolled into *ficelles, baguettes* and *pains* and placed on the canvas-lined shelves for storage in the fermentation locker. The shelves are rolled in to the fermentation locker and stored for tomorrow's bread. The whole process is complete by about 10:30 a.m, but the day is not yet over. We go from the *fournil* to the *pâtisserie* to begin making tomorrow's *croissants, pains au chocolat, eclairs, gateaux, tartes, religieuses, etc.* After watching Philippe mix thirty-two eggs and a forklift load of butter with sugar and chocolate, I begin to understand why those creamy fillings taste so good. I think the *pâtisserie* is a separate story by itself. My arteries are clogging up by just watching the fabrication of these delights. Thank God for the French Paradox. We share a bottle of wine to cleanse our arteries and feed our spirits. All is finished by one o'clock in the afternoon. Philippe is all grins. He says that he loves his work even though it is a hard life. He is only thirty-eight years old but he has been baking bread for twenty-four years. Although many young people in France are acquiring the restless discontent of Americans, most of the French seem incredibly content with their lives. I am certainly content with mine.

Steak and Kidney Pudding

Across the broad waters of the Langeron River in the commune of Villavard, the last tribe of English holds tenaciously to the vendômois domain that Henry II and Richard the Lionhearted fought for nearly one thousand years ago. It is hard to call those Plantagenêt Kings of England anything but French since they lived, fought and died in France. But it is not hard to call Clive Harrison an Englishman. Even though he has lived in France with his French wife, Denise, for twenty years, he still enjoys English cuisine. We were invited to enjoy that same cuisine last Saturday night. What could be more English than steak and kidney pudding? When prepared in a French kitchen by a master French cook and served with a nine year-old Bordeaux, well, it is very, very English.

Steak and Kidney Pudding

Preparation time—20 minutes
Cooking time—4 hours and 30 minutes
Ingredients:
For the filling:
1 pound of skirt beef stewing steak
4 ounces of ox kidney
1 ounce of seasoned flour
1 onion, peeled and chopped
For the pastry:
8 ounces self-raising flour
1/2 level teaspoon salt
4 ounces of shredded suet
8 tablespoons of cold water

Directions:

Cut steak in 1-inch cubes. Remove skin, core and fat from kidney then cut into 1/2 inch pieces. Coat the steak with seasoned flour.

Sieve flour and salt for pastry into a bowl. Stir in suet, and then add enough water to make fairly soft dough. Roll out two-thirds of pastry to a circle large enough to line a greased, 2-pint pudding basin. Roll out the remaining pastry to a circle the size of the top of the basin.

Put steak, kidney, and onion in alternate layers in basin, and then add sufficient water to come within 1-inch of the top of the basin. Moisten edges of pastry lid and press firmly on top. Cover with lid of greaseproof paper, and then cover with a lid of foil; both pleated to allow for expansion. Steam or boil the pudding for 4 1/2 hours, topping up with boiling water as necessary.

Serve with potatoes, carrots, Brussels sprouts, broccoli, fresh home-made butter from a local farm, French bread and numerous bottles of nine-year old Bordeaux. Follow with cheese, lardy cake, and French pressed coffee. Finally, finish with Denise's homemade sloe gin. I love the Fenglish.

Winter Foods

Winter foods evoke the strongest memories. The weather drives everyone inside but it is food that bonds them together. When I wrote about steak and kidney pudding, some English friends wrote back about the memories that the recipe brought them. Here is what Virginia Harding wrote:

I always enjoy receiving your Tales from the Loir, but am moved particularly on this occasion to comment on one thing lacking from the Steak and Kidney Pudding! My very English mother used to wrap a clean linen napkin round the bowl or 'pudding basin' she made it in, and secure it with pins or safety pins, before taking it to the table. This manages to make the dish even more English than it is already! Also she always had a jug of spare liquid or 'gravy' beside her when she served it, as there is a lot of steak and kidney in it, you need to pour in more liquid as you serve and stir within the suet crust! Yum yum, I do miss her!

Then my friend Bob Dart brought back some memories for me by writing about the old custom in the South of eating cornbread, turnip greens and black-eyed peas on New Year's Day. Here is what he wrote:

Shredded suet? Ox kidney? Can you get those at the IGA on St. Simons? I cooked a huge pot of turnip greens and roots and chopped up ham and the ham hock last week and I'm looking forward to black-eyed peas and rice and chopped raw onions while watching bowl games on New Year's Day. I think about you whenever I read about the search for bin Laden in the caves.

Sandy Wells responded from South Georgia with this story:

All your letters are great, and I really envy y'all. Don't forget the REAL Hoppin' John. Down here people tend to eat black-eyed peas, but I was raised in Sav'h on Mom's Low Country Hoppin' John (for New Year's Day good luck). It is made with tiny red peas and hog jowl and rice.

I used to go to the SpeeDee Market on Gloucester St., where the sign in the window said "goat" and, at this time of year, "red peas" (they told me they drove to Montezuma, Ga. to get them [and these are dried peas!]. Later they had 'em at IGA, and now I have to go to Harvey's in Brunswick to find them.

You first cook some meaty hog jowl (actually Mom always watched fat content, so she'd use a little jowl for good luck and then maybe a meaty ham hock) in water for a bit, then add washed, soaked peas and chopped onions, some salt and pepper. Cook for a while until peas are done. Take your rice steamer (all OLD folk from the Low Country have them) and cook rinsed rice with the liquid from the peas. When that's about done, gently spoon in (with slotted spoon) the peas and meat from the jowl, and from hock, if you have it.

It's delicious. Like a Pilau (which Mom pronounces "perlow"). I've had similar rice dishes in the Bahamas. It gets better with time, too. I still have to make a bit of it along with collards for New Year's. I just dole it out to neighbors for good luck.

Speaking of collards, Nelson and I saw what looked exactly like them (and I finally picked and tasted it, and it tasted like collards) growing in fields in France. But we couldn't figure out what they do with it or what the name of it was. Have you noticed anything like that?

The weather here finally feels like Christmas and oyster roast season. Still wouldn't mind being over there for champagne, oysters and foie gras. Had a cool thing at a party here before Christmas: Oyster Shooters. They took individual single oysters and put one each in shot glasses with a little cocktail sauce, then served 'em on a silver tray. You'd just down a shooter and replace the empty shot glass on the tray as they passed them. Guess it requires a person in the kitchen opening the oysters (and a large supply of shot glasses) as they really did taste like they had just been shucked. Later in the evening I heard that they added a little vodka to each one. Glad I was already gone.

Living in France creates a whole new set of memories for the holidays. While helping Aprille set up a display of her sculptures in the garage of Gaston Cottenceau for the annual village Christmas market, we were invited for an aperitif in Gaston's basement bar and twelfth century wine cellar. He had a roaring fire in the fireplace with a large turkey spinning from the mantel in front of the fire. A pan underneath was catching the dripping fat to be used later with chestnuts to make a sauce. I have not seen a turkey cooked like this before but chickens and leg of lamb are an everyday event in the caves of Lavardin. Cooking meat on a string in the fireplace is an old tradition here and it works so well that I often wonder why other regions have not adopted it.

The Christmas market also generates its own traditions. I have attended Christmas markets in Munich, Germany, and was impressed with the hundreds of artisans selling handmade Christmas tree ornaments. The streets were full of people shopping until late in the evening for the special tree ornaments found only in that area of the world. Hot-spiced wine was very popular but food was not a big part of the German markets.

Lavardin's Christmas market is different from the ones in Munich. There are a few stands selling some Christmas ornaments and decorations but the emphasis of this market is on food and wine. It takes place during the second weekend in December and it is usually cold but the crowds of people flocking to our picturesque village are not deterred. Just in front of Aprille's stand, the winemakers, Vincent and Sylvie Norguet have a table for tasting their new vintages. Next door is a stand for the fresh, salty oysters from the Charente-Maritime coast of France. This is a strategic location for me because everyone passes by to take a glass of the dry, tangy chenin vintage with the first dozen. All day long I hear the magic words, *Tu veux un verre?* as friends and neighbors pass by. If one tires of oysters the neighboring stands offer goat cheese, various meats, pâtés and terrines of ostrich meat, charcuterie of every description and honey from the farm of our new Mayor, Gerard Allaire.

The wine is too cold for Aprille so I go down to the center of town where *vin chaud* spiced with cinnamon is offered along with roasted chestnuts, *mergeuez* sausages, French fries, and *crêpe*s. There is also a *boulanger*, a *patissier* and a *confiseur* for bread, pastries and chocolates. I purchase a coffee for Aprille and a cornet of roasted chestnuts for myself. The cold weather makes us hungry but a dinner at the Caveau Restaurant is planned for after the market so we skip the sausages and French fries.

At nine o'clock we close our stand and walk down to the Caveau for a dinner of *choucroute garnie*. Choucroute is the Alsatian specialty that we call sauerkraut, but in France it is much more than shredded cabbage when the *garnie* word is used. It is a virtual feast of pork, ham, bacon, and various sausages placed on a bed of choucroute. An occasional potato is thrown on to represent the carbohydrate food group and sometimes carrots add a little color. The sauerkraut itself is cooked in Champagne or Alsatian wine and has a sour/sweet taste that compliments the pork products. It is usually served with beer or a dry white wine from the Alsace. Choucroute is unique as the only French dish where beer is tolerated. However, most French opt for the white wine. I tried both and can report that they both work well.

Choucroute garnie
Ingredients:
5 pounds fresh sauerkraut
1/3 cup chopped bacon

4 squares of bacon rind, 1 1/2-inches each (optional)
3 cloves garlic, chopped
1/2 bottle dry white wine
2 tablespoons juniper berries
1 teaspoon whole black peppercorns
4 cloves
12 ounce chunk of unsmoked bacon
4 each of 4 different sausages (frankfurter, bratwurst, knockwurst, etc.)
1 smoked veal tongue
Directions:

Immerse the sauerkraut in a large bowl filled with cold water, and soak for 15 minutes. While sauerkraut is soaking, place the chopped bacon and the optional bacon rind in a heavy, oven proof pot over high heat. Sauté for 1 minute. Turn heat to medium-low, add the garlic and sauté for another minute. Pre-heat oven to 325 degrees.

Squeeze the sauerkraut dry, reserving 1 cup of the soaking water and add the sauerkraut to the pot. Stir well to blend with bacon. Add the reserved cup of soaking water, the white wine, the juniper berries, the peppercorns and the cloves. Bring to boil on top of stove and boil until the liquid has almost evaporated (about 20-30 minutes). Imbed the meats in the sauerkraut, cover the pot and cook in the oven until the meats are hot, about 30 minutes. Serve on a large platter

Winter Solstice

As we board the 7 a.m. train for Paris, I wonder what people back home are doing for the holidays. I picture Naugahyde recliners, cans of Budweiser, and long drowsy naps in front of the television during the annual Enron North-South Bowl or the East-West Shrine Bowl Classic. Not this year. We are establishing our own new traditions. It is called installation art and I am participating in a small way. It is the 21st of December, winter solstice, the shortest day of the year. It is below freezing and a stiff wind is blowing. We head for the Louvre to commence the installation. Aprille has spent the last two months cutting lines and paragraphs from *Pascal's Pensées* into strips. The idea is to place the strips throughout the twenty arrondissements of Paris and record the event with video and photographs. The place where one's artistic talent is shown, aside from coming up with the idea, is in selecting the right place to photograph one of the pithy axioms. It can be a trash can, a pool of water at the Louvre or a mirror reflecting the surroundings.

We get to the Pyramid of the Louvre by 8:30 a.m. but it is still dark and still very cold. Rain would be the only thing to make the situation worse. As Aprille sets up her tripod and camera, it begins to rain. I am not sure I am cut out to be an artist. After an hour of freezing to death, I elect to abandon the project for a local cafe serving petit déjeuner. Aprille will push on for another ten hours, traveling in a spiral from the Louvre in the first arrondissement to the other nineteen, or until midnight. She is loaded with a backpack containing a computer, cameras, cassettes, disks, tripods and a large container with the strips of paper containing the quotes.

The idea, as I understand it, is that a book or a poem is a piece of art that is in a way cut into to strips as it is read. The words and lines are randomly stored in one's mind like strips of paper that the mind can never assimilate again and eventually loses, like Aprille's strips blowing off with the wind. The seventeenth century French philosopher-mathematician, Blaise Pascal, made a similar observation in his book, *Pascal's Pensées*. Aprille read this book one Sunday morning while I was playing checkers with myself. This is what happens when you live in a cave in France. One's basic nature is revealed.

It is hard to believe that anyone could actually read the whole book, but I know that she did. This is not a pamphlet. It is several hundred pages long and the plot sucks. It is actually a treatise on religion but it rambles a field sometimes. Here is a quote:

Which is more reliable? Moses or China.

As I leave the hotel to find Aprille again, a man stops me and asks where he can find rue Surcouf. I take this as a good omen because I know the location of one street in Paris and a stranger asks me where it can be found. When I rejoin Aprille again at 6:00 o'clock in the evening it is already dark again, but she has taken thousands of pictures and astonished hundreds of Parisians. During the short time that I am with her, I hear people saying, *c'est fou, qu'est-ce qu'elle fait?* and *c'est bizarre.* I am not sure that I want to be associated with the project, so I hang back as we head toward the Eiffel Tower on the small back streets, looking for that special place to leave a quote. When Aprille steps in a pile of dog shit, I see my chance to participate in the project. I put one of Pascal's best in the deformed pile and take a photograph. I immediately feel that special sensation that only artists feel when they have finished a masterpiece. It is sheer genius.

We finish taking pictures of a quote stuck to a yellow letterbox at the Eiffel Tower and head toward the Champs Elysees. I am beginning to tire and suggest that we go to dinner. Aprille is totally exhausted but wants to push on. I follow for a while longer but my whining is messing with her *chi* and she can no longer find the places to put the strips of paper. We cross the Seine and find a lighted place in front of a dress shop where the picture taking continues, but it is getting late and fewer people are stopping to gape. Aprille finally agrees to give up because it is dark, cold and starting to rain again. Also she wants to go see the pictures she has taken so she can plan the next project that will be on June 22 or the summer solstice.

As we head back to the hotel, I think about all the cards and letters from friends and relatives talking about their children and the holidays. It brings a good feeling. It is nice to know that there are fires in the hearths and another adventure around the corner.

Eat, Drink, Sleep...

Food and wine are traditions in France the whole year round, but during the holiday season the feasts are extraordinary. We spent Christmas weekend in Nantes where we enjoyed the traditional cuisine of the region and the fellowship of friends. We had oysters, shrimp, raclettes, *pommes de terre aux lardons, foie gras*, duck, various cheeses and lots of muscadet. When we got back to Lavardin, we had *fondue chinoise, pot au feu*, salmon grilled over the fire, and *filet de sandre au beurre blanc*. We drank Champagne, Vouvray petillant, and the wines of Chinon, Bourgeuil, Quincy, Sancerre and *côteaux du Vendômois*. But all of these delights are only a warm-up for New Year's day dinner at chez Séguin.

The subtitle of my first book, *Eat, Drink, Sleep...*, came from one of these Séguinian experiences. It was about two years ago, while spending a weekend with Gilbert and Ginette Séguin, that I heard their son, Patrice, say *"mange, bois, dors....mange, bois, dors... Ça c'est nous."* We have been to many of these five-hour marathons on Sunday afternoon, but New Year's Day is special and so is our dinner for the first day of the third millennium.

We arrive at the Séguin's home in the small village of Meslay at noon. After the traditional greeting of kisses and hand shakes, we all gather in the living room for aperitifs and *amuses bouches*. Our friend Michel Desoeuvres is one of the guests and the source of today's wine. Michel has decided to stop collecting wine and has been in the process of emptying his cellar for some years. For the aperitifs he brought a sweet white wine from Bordeaux much like a Sauternes. The label reads Domaine de Ballan, 1989, Premières Côtes de Bordeaux. Gilbert pours the wine while Ginette brings in the *amuses bouches* which include olives, crackers, pickled mussels, cauliflower, tomato slices, mushrooms and several sauces for dipping.

We spend about an hour sipping this golden nectar and preparing our palates for the first course.

We move to the dining room where Ginette has set the table with nametags on little, ladybug-shaped boxes of specialty chocolates and lotto cards. There are small bowls of chocolates spread around the table for anyone who gets hungry between courses. I don't believe that this has ever happened at Ginette's table, but she has the base covered just in case.

The first course is mackerel rillets served in small bowls. Gilbert pours a sauvignon from the Loir and Cher with the rillets. This dry grassy wine is perfect for the fish and even better with the oysters from l'ile d'Oré (*sic*) which is served next. The oysters are served raw, chilled and already opened and stacked on sliver platters. There are so many oysters that Ginette is having difficulty finding volunteers to finish the last couple dozen. I do my share and Gilbert lends support by pouring a Vin d'Alsace, Tokay Pinot Gris, 1998, from the domain of J.L. Bucher.

I am ready to move on to the *plat principal* but Ginette is still serving seafood. She brings out individual plates of *saumon sauvage fumé* sprinkled with dill and decorated with caviar in a cup made from the bottom of an artichoke. Gilbert pours a Bordeaux rosé, 1998, from the Domain de Ballan for the smoked salmon and a *petit verre* of vodka for the caviar. If we could stop here, I would go away saying that I ate and drank way too much so I don't know how to describe what we actually consumed today.

The principal dish is roasted pintade from the farm of Michel Desoeuvres. It is served with a stuffing made from pork and chestnuts. There is also a large patter of green beans and mushrooms (*pleurotes*), which are served with two kinds of sauces. We are offered three kinds of Bordeaux with this course. There is a Medoc, 1985, from the domain of Baron Phillippe. There is a Château des Rochers, 1983, Montagne-Saint Emilion and the final choice is a Château de Mornon, 1995, Premières Côtes de Blaye.

The next course is a large platter of cheeses and mâche salad served in a large wooden bowl made from the trunk of an olive tree. Dessert is a kind of ice cream cake and a plate of cookies called *papillons*. This is all followed by coffee and chocolates. Afterwards, Gilbert insists that I try a special brandy called Fine Bretagne with the domain name of Séguin on the bottle.

It is now five o'clock and already getting dark outside. During the warmer months of the year, we would normally all go for a long walk after a meal like this but it is cold and raining so we play cards and watch television to let everything settle a bit. About an hour later Ginette notices that we are growing feint with hunger and starts to set the table again. Gilbert opens a bottle of Champagne and we toast the New Year and *la fraternité*.

At around seven o'clock, Ginette orders us back to the table for a little snack. She brings out a large bowl of fish soup with toast, rouille and cheese for sprinkling on top. Gilbert tells us to put the rouille and the cheese in the soup. I have always eaten the rouille on the toast so this is new to me. The soup is thick, hot and tasty. Ginette explains that she made the soup using six different types of fish. She also says that she used a kilo of each type of fish. That adds up to about thirteen pounds of fish. While Ginette is serving the soup, Gilbert is pouring a rosé from Provence along with the remains of the various Bordeaux not yet consumed. Aprille has already switched to a fine *eau mineral de* Cévennes called Quézac. Another mineral water without gas is also available called Hepare.

The next course is a rabbit terrine made with pistachio nuts. Afterwards, we have cheese, salad and more of the papillons. Then more coffee and chocolates to finish the day. It is ten o'clock.

Festival of Saint Vincent

Saint Vincent is the patron saint of the *vignerons* (winemakers). The Festival of Saint Vincent takes place every year on the 22nd of January. The 22nd of January represents a crucial period in the annual cycle. It is near the winter solstice and the passage from the state of dormancy to the state of resurrection of the vines. This probably represents the pagan origins of the festival. It is also the time in many vineyards when the vines are trimmed and cut. The festival has many variations across France, but it is basically a religious celebration in the wine growing regions that has become more and more of a community celebration. After the religious ceremony on 22 January, the drinking and eating begins and lasts up to four days in some regions. The parties only stop to milk the cows as one historian wrote. Sometimes there is a ceremony to induct new members who are required to chug-a-lug 50 cl (2/3 bottle) of wine without stopping.

Last year the local cabinet maker was inducted and was required to drink two of these glasses because it was the year 2000. The rest of the ceremony involves eating, drinking, dancing, and many speeches extolling the virtues of wine and the wine growers. The speeches include stories like the one concerning Cardinal de Berry who lived in the seventeenth century and was a protégé of Madame de Montespan. It is said that he served only a very fine meursault at mass to prevent his flock from making faces in front of Jesus.

I missed the festival last year because of other obligations. This year I was invited to three different festivals but I was only able to attend one. The village of Saint Rimay held its festival a week earlier this year so as not to conflict with the festival of other villages. Here is the menu for the Festival. It says it all.

Saint Rimay
Menu
De La Saint Vincent
13 janvier 2001
BEUVEZ TOUJOURS NE MOURREZ JAMAIS
(Drink forever and never die)
(Rabelais)

The vigneron from Vouvray sitting across the table from me told me that this is the devise (motto) for the Chinon region of France. The devise for Vouvray is Je rejouis les coeurs (I gladden the heart). I have to admit that my heart has been gladdened many times by a glass of Vouvray and I drink Chinon each night and am not dead.
President: DE TANDT Raymond
Vice-Président: VIAU Jacques

Bon
Appétit
VINS
COLOMBELLE (Blanc)

SAUMUR CHAMPIGNY
BORDEAUX
MENU
Apéritif
This a kir with kiwi and strawberries in the bottom of the glass.
Assiette Spriritueuse
This was a salad of noix de Saint Jacques on a bed of mâche with a mustard sauce.
Pavé de Sandre au Beurre d'Orange
This is the first course. Sandre is a perch like fresh water fish that is common in France.
Sorbet aux poires
This is supposed to clean the palette.
Biche aux Airelles
Deer meat with mushrooms. Deer meat in France is as tender as veal. I don't know why.

Salade
Fromages
Gâteau aux Trois Chocolats
Café
Digestif
Mousseux

This was about a six-hour dinner with a lot of wine, songs and jokes. The singing starts about the time of the fish course and continues until the end of the dinner. From time to time, someone will stand up and start singing, *a cappella*. Others stand up and tell jokes. The singing and jokes continue throughout the meal. Here is the refrain from one of the songs about cheese. This song has many verses and goes on for several minutes but I was only able to capture the refrain.

Etoile de crèmes, mon bon camembert
C'est toi qui j'aime comme dessert
Apres le potage, après les fayotes
Roi des fromage, de tous les mets
T'es bien le plus beau.

The songs are generally traditional French songs that everyone seems to recognize. The jokes are hard to follow. Language problems show up clearly when someone tells a joke. I can tell from the inflections that a joke has been told and it is time to laugh but I am faking it every time. But there is no faking it with the songs. I am completely charmed to be a part of this ancient French tradition.

The festival of Saint Vincent is many things. It is a religious festival and, at the same time, a secular celebration. It is a wine festival and a festival primarily for men but also a community event. However it is celebrated, Saint Vincent appears in it as a prominent symbol and it is an important event for the wine growers.

Tête de Veau

Many people think that the Gods punished Prometheus for giving Mankind fire but this is not true. He was punished for deceiving the Gods when they were trying to decide which part of cattle to give to Man and which part to keep for themselves. Prometheus tricked them into selecting the head, fat and sinew of cattle while leaving the better cuts for humans. They were so angry about their loss that they chained Prometheus to a mountain top and sent an eagle to eat his liver everyday.

In medieval France, the Lords of the manors made the same mistake. They had the first choice of newly butchered cattle. They always chose the head. It was symbolic of their position and power over their feudal minions. The peasants were left with the steaks, chops and roasts while the *Seigneur* feasted on *tête de veau*. Perhaps it is the symbolism of status and

194

power that continues to make this dish so popular in France. It is not the taste.

Here are the directions for preparing tête de veau:
Rip the face off of a baby cow. Remove the m eat from the jaw and roll it up in the face. Tie it all up with string and place it is a large pot with water, a carrot, an onion, chopped garlic, bouquet garni, salt, pepper and a little vinegar. Simmer for two hours, then remove, drain and cut in slices. Place slices on warm plates then lightly moisten each spongy, tasteless mass with a special vinaigrette sauce.

I am in inveterate Francophile, at least as far as food and wine are concerned. I eat snails, frog legs, duck liver, blood sausage, small birds, bunny rabbits and Mr. Ed *au poivre*, but I have a problem with *tête de veau*. Ever since the movie *Silence of the Lambs*, the idea of eating *tête de veau* has not appealed to me. In addition to the psychological problem, there is the real threat of *vache folle* (mad cow) disease. Mad cow has not been a big problem in the States but in Europe and Great Britain it has been devastating. Last year people in France stopped eating beef for fear of contacting the disease. I was so concerned about the problem that I saved the following newspaper article and pasted it over my desk for future reference:

> *Mad cow disease, or bovine spongiform encephalopathy, is believed to be caused by a mutated protein that is <u>transmitted through eating pieces of the brain or nervous system</u> of an infected animal. It is linked to a human brain- wasting disease, variant Creutzfeld Jakob Disease, that has so far killed 102 people in Britain since 1995, three in France, one in Ireland and one in Hong Kong.*

When my friend Maurice Cheron called last year to invite us to have *tête de veau* at a dinner party in his cave, I had no idea what it was. To my way of thinking the head of a baby cow would have to be brains and eyeballs. Maurice had been bragging about how good his *tête de veau* was for over a year so there was no way to refuse. When I was served a plate, I was genuinely surprised. It was a white spongy substance that had very little taste except for the special vinaigrette sauce that is put on top.

I later asked a friend about the wisdom of eating *tête de veau* in light of the problem with mad cow disease. He told me that it was not a problem because *tête de veau* is just the face and jaw of the cow and does not include the brains or nervous system.

With that concern past me, I am ready to try it again without the prejudice of death hanging over my head. After all, it is the favorite dish of Jacques Chirac, the President of the Republic, and everyone tells me it is a special delicacy. I am in luck because our friends Zoulika and Emmanuel have decided to hire Maurice to do his *tête de veau* at their dinner party. Maurice's dinners are the classic French eat 'til it hurts marathons. They start at noon and usually finish around midnight. There is a short break around six o'clock but I suspect the break is just to wash the dishes for the final leg of the event.

We are fourteen at the party and everyone is oohing and aahing about the *tête de veau*. Maurice is grinning from ear to ear because he is rightly proud of his cuisine. I learn from the other dinner guests that *tête de veau* is a special treat for the French that everyone seems to love. I find that I am somewhat of a follower. If everyone says it is good and a rare treat to be enjoyed at every opportunity, I am beginning to think that it is my favorite dish too. I even ask for a second helping.

I compliment Maurice profusely and to show him how well read I am, I inform him that *tête de veau* is the favorite dish of Jacques Chirac but that the President prefers to eat it with the brains, the tongue and the glands that are attached to the tongue. Maurice curves his finger in a sign to follow him over to the pot. He opens the cover and pulls the contents out of the pot with a large ladle. It is the whole head of a cow with brains, tongue and gangling things that must be the dreaded nervous system. Bon appetit.

La Chandeleur
(Candlemas)

When Madam Lallier invited Aprille and me for *crêpes* at four o'clock in the afternoon, I had no idea what *Chandeleur* was. It is more commonly called the day of the *crêpes* but it is always celebrated on February 2. For hundreds of years the French have celebrated *Chandeleur* by preparing *crêpes* in the afternoon before it gets dark. Madame Lallier told me that the tradition is to flip the first *crêpe* with one hand while holding a gold coin in the other. If one succeeds in this task, wealth and good health will follow for the rest of the year. In former times the *crêpes* were prepared over the fireplace and it was an exciting day for the children of the household. After greasing a frying pan with lard, it would be heated over the fireplace until hot enough to pour the batter for the first *crêpe*. As everyone prepared for the acrobatic flip with one hand on the gold, the youngest child would be sent outside as a joke to catch the *crêpe* when it came out of the chimney. It is a great day for children because these *crêpes* are made with eggs, butter, milk, sugar and filled with homemade preserves and jelly. Of course, no one eats anything in France without something to drink and here the tradition is to drink cider with *crêpes*. Madame Lallier serves us cider from Normandy and tells us that a lot of cider is traditionally made here in the Loir and Cher, but that it is a little bit sharper tasting than the great ciders of Brittany and Normandy.

Chandeleur was originally a pagan festival celebrated by the Romans to honor the dead. On a certain day of the year and during funerals, everyone stood watch with candles and torches to pay homage to Pluto and the other gods of Hell. It became a Christian celebration in the fifth century

197

when it was adopted by Pope Gélase I as a substitute for the pagan festival of *Lupercales* that honored the Roman God Pan, the god of flocks and herds. In the sixth century Pope Vigile instituted the festival to replace the festival of Proserpine (Persephone in Greek mythology). *Chandeleur* eventually became the day of celebration of the presentation of Christ in the Temple and the purification of Mary. During this ceremony many candles were lit and blessed (*Chandeleur* means festival of the candles). During the middle ages, processions of people carrying lit candles went through the fields and vineyards. There were also processions from the church to the homes of the marchers. The belief was that if your candle went out before you reached home, you would die during the year.

The more sinister origins of *Chandeleur* are far behind us and the festival is now celebrated in the afternoon before the sun goes down. But it is dark by the time we leave the sixteenth century home of Madame Lallier. She tells us that her home is too young to be classed as a national heritage, but I feel the weight of the middle ages here. Perhaps it is the stained glass windows, the six-foot high fireplace and the huge wooden beams that give gives me the sense of the past. Or maybe it is just the feeling that one gets when people still practice traditions that are hundreds of years old.

Conclusion

As I climb the steep hill to the plain above our cave, I see two small deer playing like puppies among the bails of hay in the freshly cut wheat field. As I stop and stare at this unusual scene, a large hare, blinded by my immobility, runs directly at me before a slight movement alerts it to its proximity to danger. It stands frozen only a few feet away and stares for an eternity before bounding back into the stubble of the wheat field. A herd of cows in the enclosure on my left gather at the fence and stare at me as only cows can do. I begin to think that I am wrong about deep France not being a place.

This scene certainly looks like deep France, but it has nothing to do with tradition, authenticity or the spirit of the people. It is just nature. I started with the belief that it was just something old and quaint. After living in its milieu, I came to believe that it is also tied to the rhythm of life and the change of seasons. I now see it separately in *la terre*.

While leaning on the fence considering this thought, one of those small, round hobbit-like farmers drives up in his little French truck and stops to shoot the breeze. We lean on the fence, stare at the cows and discuss the weather. I realize that I am wrong. This place is not just nature. It is nature with a deep France personality. This is his land and his animals and they are uniquely, or perhaps typically, molded to his personality. The fields, the cows, the deer and the wild hares are all part of the personality of this man and they are all a part of the formula making this place deep France. I now know the answer but I am not sure.

Appendix

French National Tourist Office
628 Fifth Ave.
New York, New York 10020

Alliance Française Val de Loire
21, place Saint-Martin
41100 Vendôme, France
Telephone: 33 (0) 2 54 73 13 20
Fax: 33 (0) 2 54 73 23 20
E-mail: alliancefrançaise@mail.dotcom.fr
http://www.mygale.org/08/afvdl

Office de Tourisme
Hôtel du Saillant- Parc Ronsard
41100 Vendôme, France
Telephone: 33 (0) 2 54 77 05 07
Fax: 33 (0) 2 54 73 20 81
E-mail: ot.Vendome@wanadoo.fr
http://www.tourisme.fr

Ville de Vendôme
Hôtel de Ville-Parc Ronsard
41100 Vendôme, France
Telephone: 33 (0) 2 54 77 25 33
Fax: 33 (0) 2 54 80 21 64

Office de Tourisme
16, Place Clemenceau
41800 Montoire-Sur-Le-Loir, France
Telephone: 33 (0) 2 54 85 23 30
Fax: 33 (0) 2 54 85 23 87

Résurgence en Vendômois
9, impasse St. Pierre Lamothe
41100 Vendôme, France

Alliance Française de Jacksonville
112 West Adams Street, #1402
Jacksonville, FL 32202
RVDUSS@aol.com

Jacksonville Sister Cities Association
Room 1400, City Hall
220 East Bay Street
Jacksonville, FL 32202

Mairie de Lavardin
2 impasse St. Genest
41800 Lavardin

William and Aprille Glover
2000-1 Hendricks Ave, PMB #7
Jacksonville, FL 32207
www.aprille.net
www.cavelife.net
gloverwh@aol.com